Spiritual
KNOWINGS

CAROLINE ROLLO

First published in paperback by
Michael Terence Publishing in 2024
www.mtp.agency

Copyright © 2024 Caroline Rollo

Caroline Rollo has asserted the right to be identified as the author of this work in accordance with the Copyright, Designs and Patents Act 1988

ISBN 9781800947719

No part of this publication may be reproduced, stored in a retrieval system, or transmitted, in any form or by any means, electronic, mechanical, photocopying, recording or otherwise, without the prior permission of the publisher

Cover image
www.123rf.com

Cover design
Copyright © 2024 Michael Terence Publishing

Michael Terence
Publishing

Contents

1: Introduction 1
2: My Mum 9
3: My Dad 19
4: Bushey 24
5: My Sister, Maruja 39
6: Bushey in the 50s 64
7: Big School 70
8: Watford in the 60s 80
9: Life for Me in the 70s 84
10: Wedding Plans Go Ahead 98
11: The 90s 108
12: Millenium Year 2000 109
13: Finding Spiritual Knowings 111
14: My Work for Spirit Finally Begins 116

MY OWN WORKSHOP 123

15: History 124
16: Talking Spirit 127
17: Types of Mediumships 132
18: Spirit Guides 151
19: Angels 172

20: Chakras and Auras	178
21: Vortexes and Ley Lines	190
22: Orbs and Rods	199
23: Signs of Spirit to Look For	201
24: The Third Eye Awakening	206
25: Healing	210
26: The Dark Side	215
27: Working on Vibrations	219
28: One to One Readings	220
29: My Meditations	224
30: My Poetry	231
31: Finally	237

1
Introduction

I have been spiritual since birth and was compelled to write this book at this stage of my life. Having worked for Spirit over the last twenty-five years, the time is right for me to share my thoughts, my feelings and experiences. I have learnt so much in this time and feel it just might help someone who may be starting out on their own spiritual journey to make sense of it all. We all seek inner peace at some point and no matter how many people we have around us, inside our own headspace, we sometimes feel lost or lonely, but to have Spirit with us and to be able to feel their presence with that well-being, changes everything. Just to have the knowledge that we are never alone.

Spiritualism is there for each and every one of us to tap into if we so desire, enabling us to sense, feel and in some cases see Spirit visually in solid form or through visualisation from our third eye. Spirit will always help us in difficult times, giving help along the way. When we feel we are drowning in emotions of sadness, anxiety or uncertainty, Spirit is there to love and guide us. I will tell you what to expect and what signs to look for when Spirit is close.

Maybe it's because at the time of writing this book, being in my 70s I now need to leave something behind, even if that something is just for my grandchildren to read. I need to tell them and others who I am and what I have tried to achieve in my life's journey. People will find their own way in life and will have their own beliefs, whilst walking their destined paths, that's as it should be. However, I want people to know what my faith has done and given to me and I would very much like my grandchildren to know and to be comforted in the fact, I will never leave them spiritually. Life does go on and I will be there for them should I ever be needed, as indeed my loved ones in the spirit world are always here for me. My belief is that in life, we are drawn to certain people, books and places or situations to find answers, the learning curves and moral compasses kick in. This book is not meant to change your faith in any way, whatever you believe in that's fine, but perhaps it will change the way you think about dealing with life and how you cope with others around you in everyday situations. We are living in very challenging times, it's good to be positive about the future and the way forward.

There is a great deal of responsibility that goes with being a Spiritual Medium especially sharing thoughts and experiences from Spirit World with others and when passing on personal messages, you have to get it right it's very important not only for you, but for the person in Spirit that is giving the message, both need to feel relaxed in the knowledge that you as the medium respect their privacy and are merely a messenger. The code of conduct for me is what is learnt in a reading, stays in a reading.

All Spiritual Mediums have their own unique take on events giving us opinions on things and I respect them all, as we all work in different ways. It takes courage to stand up in front of an audience in a church hall or theatre and say you're connecting and talking to people that have passed over. In life there is not one of us that can say, I have no regrets thinking back, I wish I myself had handled certain situations differently, but it's how we intend to move forward that counts. We do learn from mistakes, but we can also learn to accept we have made them, and how to move on and live with them afterwards.

Yes, Spiritualism can teach us to be tolerant of others and also to throw love at things where possible, but it also teaches us when its right to walk away from certain situations or from certain people who can be toxic and those who can drain us of our energy, giving us their bad vibes and negativity, when we come across such people and situations which may be in our everyday surroundings such as work or friends or even family, we must learn to reflect this negativity back and not take any of their personal bad energy onboard ourselves. My method is to have a large imaginary mirror in front of me, looking into it and then turning it around to face the person who is being so unkind, it's my way of dealing with it, reflecting all that bad, nasty or unkind energy back via that imaginary mirror and saying in my head, 'Your problem, not mine'. It gives you strength in character as we all need a little help sometimes. No one should be allowed to mess with your head and no one ever really knows what we are personally thinking in our own headspace, so we can be in total control of our own minds, our consciousness, at all times that's vitally important.

Working in Spiritualist Churches and Halls mainly around the Herts, Beds and Bucks areas, I found it to be a sheer joy for me meeting many wonderful people, who would tell me of their own experiences and strange happenings and the wonder of spirit world. It's fascinating, each person having their own unique story to tell, it was a comfort to me and very rewarding to hear others going through similar experiences. People would ask if I got tired or felt drained after doing this work, but I never have, for the most part it was very uplifting. However, many times a person would only get a ten-minute slot with me in a church service or at a physic fair it usually lasted for twenty-minutes only, and that was not how I personally liked to work, people needed more of my time, so I eventually gave it up to work from home or travel to people's homes myself. I never advertised, but got worked from recommendations and over time I have come to realise the greatest gift you can give anyone, is your time. In many of my one-to-one sessions, having made the appointment for an hour, I would still be sitting there with people long after that hour had expired, talking about their mums or dads or loved ones who had passed over, or maybe a child that had gone to Spirit too early. Many of the people that came to me were feeling nervous or uncertain or unhappy but I was convinced most of them left feeling like a weight had been lifted from their shoulders. To have a cuppa and a chat before a reading relaxed them so that is what we did first, then when they would be ready to receive their messages. People would say to me, 'What a wonderful gift you have Caroline.' My answer was 'Yes, it's a wonderful gift, indeed, but a gift that's given to everyone it's up to us if we want to develop it or not. Simply ask Spirit for help in your head and you will receive answers.

Strong, Identifiable Evidence, from the Spirit world is essential as messages mean nothing unless they are strong and positive, as not only does it help the receiver, but the person in Spirit who is desperately trying to get their message across, as sometimes the person in spirit needs to move on into the light, and in some cases and will not rest until their message is received by their loved one. I have read for many men and women over the years who have not had the chance to say a proper goodbye after a sudden passing, heart attack or accident, or there loved one may have died abroad at the time of passing, also parents who never got the chance to hold or say to an unborn child how much they were wanted and loved. They hold that stress inside them for years and somehow after a Spiritual reading that pain is released.

A mention of a mum, dad or grandparent, in a quick message in a church, can leave people happier, but I would go home feeling quite empty, knowing that with more time I would have more to say. I wanted all my connections to be stronger and to mean so much more if that meant giving it more time so be it. I found I had a better connection and better evidence came through. If I was reading for an elderly person, you know their parents would have passed and it was not enough for me to say mum or dad is in Spirit. I would ask for my guides to give me names and to receive pictures in my mind's eye until I had that concrete evidence. That positive information and clarification which to me was essential.

I will not only tell you about my personal Spirit Guides but I will show you the evidence that they exist by way of a photo image, taken from a mirror that hung in my porch at home. This evidence I feel has helped not only me, but others that I have read for. It's one thing to tell people about Spirit Guides but something else when you can show a photo as proof. Indeed, many people that came to my home at that time saw the image of my Spirit Guide for themselves in that mirror, it would come and fade and then reappear, so beautiful. I still have that mirror today. I cannot part with it.

There are four main Spirit Guides I work with, each has a purpose to be with me, I also have a totem animal guide and Spirit people that have been friends 'or relatives they seem to come in and out of my life as needed. As you read on, I will go into detail of how they came into my life and in Part Two of the book I will explain why I believe that there are other dimensions, Portals and Vortexes around the world opening and closing all the time. Too many things have happened to me to think differently.

I am not a perfect person: far from it. I have lived the life I was supposed to. I believe it's all mapped out for us anyway. The things I have experienced were indeed meant to happen. Being hurt by people in life or indeed hurting people myself, is all part of life's pattern. We do, I'm sure, mature and grow in these situations and these experiences, although painful at the time, help us to learn life lessons. I do not, and will not judge others for their behaviour, but this wonderful thing called Spiritualism, makes us aware of our own actions in life. It has given me No fear of death for I know I would be passing over into spirit world through that wonderful dimension, existing as pure energy and I believe it will be the most wonderful experience, when my own roadmap comes to an end.

Somewhere between one and a hundred years is our life span, some are meant to reach a hundred years, others are here for a short while and others bless their little hearts just to touch base to energise and return to spirit. Everyone is here on the earth plain for the blink of an eye anyway.

In our universe, if our life was to be mapped out on a chart, it would show many high and many lows and it is how we cope with the lows that really matters. Finding out where we can draw that inner strength from, the help will be there if we ask Spirit for it. Have you ever found you were feeling low and thinking about someone and suddenly the phone would ring and it was them? Or you met someone for the first time and you took an instant liking to them immediately, while other people had the reverse effect? Do you ever wonder if you might be a little bit psychic? Well, the chances are, yes you are, and that you do have that ability! Your 6th sense just kicks in. Every experience in our life becomes a memory and as we look at something play out, sometimes it feels like it's already happened, a sort of déjà vu moment.

Understanding spiritual happenings and to know that we are never alone, makes you start to think inwardly about things, and you are in fact, being heard by Spirit so when you send messages and thoughts out from your own consciousness, the messages are indeed being received by a greater power. The feeling is just a knowing and that there is indeed much more, and all messages that are sent out by ourselves such as our wishes and hopes and prayers are being received from our own minds to that of Spirit, they are not only received and acknowledged but acted upon, just hold onto that thought. I can remember my mum saying "if you don't ask you don't get".

Coincidence can no longer be used as an excuse for something that was meant to happen, you will learn from it and in return get a deep inner understanding of it. I once contacted Colin Fry, one of the best-known Spiritual Mediums of our time he was not a close friend, just a medium I greatly admired and I respected his work, he had a television programme on at that time called Sixth Sense which fascinated me, one Saturday night I went to our local theatre in Dunstable to see him work and he later accepted me on his social media page. I asked him to send healing, if possible, to a young man that I knew needed help with healing at that time and to my amazement he answered immediately. I thanked him and followed it up by a personal question, asking him about my own mediumship and I said, 'How can I be sure what I am getting it right', he simply answered, 'It's an inner knowing', hence the name of my book. He sadly passed away after being diagnosed with cancer on the 25th August 2015 at the age of 53, such a great loss.

I have worked as a Clairsentient Medium, and it came about when I simply asked Spirit to help me do this work and whilst doing one of my first readings for a lady, I found it would just flow out of me all the information I needed. I just had to take on board what information Spirit was giving me and pass it on with confidence and integrity.

Before doing any Spiritual work, I would always first ask in my head for protection and to work in love and light, also asking my guides and helpers to draw close and for my own special Gatekeeper to stand aside, to allow me to connect and then off I went full throttle. It is a somewhat mechanical procedure, but once learnt anyone can do this. I work on a Spiritual vibration which Spirit gave out to me, and by receiving this spiritual connection I could then connect to the vibration of the person I was reading for, just our conversation and needing a yes or no answer to a question, hearing their voice, and feeling their energy was enough. I would always ask many questions in my head and allow Spirit to give me pictures through the third eye giving me clarity of who in spirit world was around them. It's not always a voice in your ear. The pictures in my head were sometimes quite odd but very clear. If I were to say to you now, whilst reading this book, stop and think of King Charles the third you have a very clear image in your mind of his face (your mind's eye if you like) or, more personally think of your father or mother, you picture them in your head immediately, well that's what it's like for me receiving thought patterns as messages and seeing the images. I don't have to think about it, I just have to receive it. Remember your first house, the one you grew up in as a child, you can clearly see it in your mind's eye, getting pictures in your head, I simply would say what I saw.

Because I don't get a voice in my ear, Spirit people contact me with their own consciousness to get their messages through. I sensed how they passed, heart attack, accident, or illness and in a couple of reading's I have done, sadly people were murdered. Most of the Spirit people I connect with love to talk about their family and would try and pass on many names. I would get bombarded with names and initials at times as they came into my head thick and fast but it was a joy to me when they were recognised. It is always a great comfort if you can indeed give the person the name, better still a nickname of their loved one directly.

There is no wrong or right way to work for Spirit as a medium. You can work the way that is best for you, as long as you feel comfortable with it. When Spirit offers you any information it should flow and you should feel relaxed with the way the information is received and be happy with that personal connection getting good results. I sometimes felt extreme changes in temperature, cold spots near me, some freezing or hot as in a flush of energy. I can also get high pitched ringing in my ears and a sort of void spaced out feeling. It's really quite odd, I need to concentrate and be on my game. When allowing Spirit to enter my personal space, it has to feel comfortable, once you are nervous and afraid, they will back off. If the Spirit people make all that effort to come through, the least you can do is listen and get it right. I find humour is the best way to get good results. If you are in a happy place, they are able to connect much easier.

I never in a million years thought I would become a Spiritual Medium myself, let alone stand up in front of people giving my own addresses which would be, notes or poems that I had written myself from the heart. I remember I went to see a medium work at the Leighton Buzzard theatre once, she was very good and, in my head, I remember thinking I would love to do that type of work Wow they heard me. It happened for me very gradually and I suppose that's how it was meant to be. So be very aware of the fact that a thought is a prayer and always heard, and in my personal experience it was acted upon. They say be careful what you ask for don't they.

This was a time in my life when I found I had more freedom as my sons were now adults which gave me the opportunity to pursue my other interests. I was now in my late forties and working full time, generally life for me was good and here I am thirty odd years later wanting to share what I have learnt and achieved over this time. Having retired now I find more and more would-be Mediums have come to me for help or advice in the workshops I do and many people who may just want to become more attuned and aware of Spirit around them. This book is a perfect way to share my ideas, thoughts and advice for what it's worth. It's written from the heart, from my many personal experiences and not from textbooks.

Reflecting back on my life I can honestly say whatever has happened to me was meant to be. Everything happens for a reason and I very strongly believe that to be true. Your past makes you who you are today, but we never stop learning. When I chat to my five young grandchildren, they teach me many new things with their own wisdom.

I have to start my journey by telling you of my family, my upbringing and my background, which include many Spiritual experiences along the way and how I started opening to Spirit properly in later years. I hope it will give you the reader enough knowledge to connect to Spirit for yourselves, giving you a little guidance and a heightened understanding of how to get started and how to do it in a safe way.

If you feel deeply that you are able to do this work or that it's your destiny to be a Medium that's wonderful, or if you just want to understand more about the Spirit world in a simple way, read on. When people say to me sometimes it's spooky or it's scary, I say be more afraid of the living, my friends. Spirit will never harm you if you live in love and light and if you have good intentions, as just by asking them for protection and guidance you will be perfectly safe. This book is an account of how I got into mediumship and to tell you my story, with my personal take on things. I have met so many wonderful spiritual people over the years here on earth in everyday life and from those in the spirit world.

Let me take you back to the very beginning.

2
My Mum

My Mum's name was Maruja Xerri, she was born in Gibraltar on the 23rd August 1923. On writing this book I realised she would have had her 100th birthday this year. She was one of six children and at the tender age of sixteen, the second world war started and this is where I shall pick up her story. In this book I shall refer to her as Mary or simply Mum.

Gibraltar is British, as in 1704, Anglo-Dutch forces captured Gibraltar from Spain during the War of the Spanish Succession. The territory was ceded to Great Britain in perpetuity under the Treaty of Utrecht in 1713, and while a lot of the British colonies gradually moved towards independence, the people of Gibraltar decided in a referendum in 1967 to remain under British rule and were loyal to Queen Elizabeth11. The vote went overwhelmingly in favour of the British. 12,138 to 44.

I have to go back to the 1939, just before the war broke out, there was only one British infantry battalion stationed on the Rock at that time however this was upped to three battalions as the second world war was imminent and the colony on Gibraltar had become one of the most important British military bases in the Mediterranean.

Gibraltar, affectionately known as The Rock, became vital to the war effort, as being a British stronghold, it provided a well defended harbour which ships could operate from, and it was a gateway to both the Atlantic and the Mediterranean seas. Gibraltar came under continued aerial bombardment once the war started so at that time it was a very dangerous place to be. Many Gibraltarian people were asked to give up their homes for the troops to use, and were told they would all be evacuated to other countries around the world for their own safety. The accommodation on Gibraltar was scarce anyway as it was such a small community, but just try to imagine how frightening that must have been for all of them, having to move away from everything they had ever known, being sent to a country they had never been to before, and not being able to see their friends and families for who knew how long, it was a scary time for all the families and for many of them it would change their lives forever.

My Grandfather in his working Garry (a horse drawn taxi) in Gibraltar

As a top military base Gibraltar grew and changed rapidly. A fully functional hospital was built under the Rock and there were miles of roads, shops and more accommodation under there. In this underground existence, the service people living under there, would hang curtains and blinds in their rooms, to make them look like proper windows, to prevent them from getting too claustrophobic. Large defensive guns stood in portals around the rock, aimed against enemy aircraft and ships. It was decided by the British government of the day, that only certain Gibraltarian civilians with vital jobs would be allowed to stay in Gib, everyone else had to leave. Old and young alike.

With a lot of fear in their hearts my mum's parents along with many other Gibraltarian families, prepared for their long journey to various destinations round the World. They could only take what they stood up in, with very little else in the way of luggage, in fact hardly anything at all, fearing the worst and having the uncertainty of what lay before them, my grandmother called Catherine Celia Xerri and my Grandfather Francisco Xerri, affectionately called Pop and their six children, mum her three sisters and two brothers, would all face this frightening time together.

In early June 1940 over thirteen thousand Gibraltarian evacuees were shipped out in all directions - some to Casablanca, some went to Jamaica others to Madeira, they were spread everywhere. A British Conservative politician Oliver Stanley, agreed to accept some evacuees into the United Kingdom. My Grandpop opted for England, and Celia (my Nanny) felt it would be safer for the family, as they had some contacts in Britain and they always took great pride in the fact that they were British.

My Grandfather, was born in Malta, he and Celia set up home after they met in Gibraltar, he worked as a Garry driver, taking tourist around the rock for a living, it was a happy carefree life bringing up their family and before the war, they had two beautiful horses, one a black shiny ex-race horse that grandpop had rescued, called bienvenidos, which means "welcome" in English, the other horse was a brown chestnut horse called Baby, which happened to be my Mum's favourite, as Baby had such a soft gentle nature. Often at the end of a working day Mum told me how she, along with her brothers and sisters, would take the horses down to Catalan Bay, and the two horses would kick about in the salt sea water. Mum would ride them bear back along the beach, what a wonderful memory for her. Gibraltar temperatures could be very hot and unbearably humid at times especially when clouds would hang over the rock: they call it The Levant. The horses loved to cool down after a day's work and they deserved a little fun also. My Mum would often talk of these days with such affection, she called them her wonderfully happy days, and how her brothers and sisters had such a happy carefree childhood. The Rock was such a small place everyone knew everyone else, it was a giant family, a safe and happy community to grow up in, and they could just enjoy their childhood, but the war was to change all that.

My Grandmother, Celia

When the time came to leave Gibraltar my Grandparents did so with heavy hearts, they also had made a heart-breaking decision to put their two lovely horses down, the alternative was unbearable. They were told that they would either have gone into Spain, probably in the bull rings, or they would have been sold as work horses, or even shot for food. It was a very black day for the family.

It was a highly emotional charged time for all the people in Gibraltar truly heart-breaking, however, those that had to leave were all told they would be safer and trusted in the Government's decision to evacuate them, also they did have the Governments assurance that after the war was over, all being well, they could return. My family was ready to head for England, my Mum, being sixteen looked at this situation as an adventure, the evacuation started.

Today, there is a history museum on The Rock that has archive photos and film footage of the departure. I first visited this excellent museum when I was in my twenties to view it for myself, and seeing the old film footage of ships being loaded and the families all gathered together for their journeys, brought back so many memories for me of what my mother had told me over the years. The Xerri family had left behind everything familiar, the sun, sea and sand, their homes, schools, businesses, family pets, their whole lives were to disappear into the distance as the ships departed. Sometimes, in many cases, loved ones would be torn apart, heading in different directions. Some like my mother never saw the Rock again.

Maruja Xerri and James William Stanners

The evacuation in 1940 and Gibraltar's history made the people of Gib who they are today, united and proud to be British, they suffered hardships and the displacements of all their families. It was such a difficult time in their history. It makes me feel very sad to think that they are not always recognised for their bravery or for their personal sacrifices they made. Their courage, help and support in the second world war was indeed a major part of history. To help in the war effort as they did was so brave. Even to this day, on September 10th each year, they celebrate being British since that referendum in 1967 when all the citizens of Gibraltar overwhelmingly voted to remain under British sovereignty it is now called Gibraltar National Day. They all come out, some form a human chain linking hands around the Rock, in a sign of protection and loyalty. I am proud to be half Gibraltarian and salute them.

HMT *Neuralia*

My family's journey started with a short trip to Rabat which is the capital of Morocco located on the Atlantic Ocean. They were told to wait there until a ship arrived to take them to England. They found their temporary accommodation in Rabat was extremely cramped with very few facilities. It prompted my Grandpop to complain as there were eight of them in one very, very tiny room. The flies and heat were unbearable with little to eat or drink and no proper toilet facilities, my grandfather was extremely concerned they would all fall ill before their journey to England had even begun.

The Chief of police in Rabat at that time got to hear of my family's predicament and went to see them personally, His name was Ashude, according to Mum he was a very tall man, slim and immaculately dressed in a white uniform, she would often comment on his handsome thin pointed face, dark hair and deep brown eyes, he undoubtedly made a big impression on her. Ashude immediately intervened and arranged to move all the family to somewhere larger and more accommodating. He took a shine to them all for some reason and kept them under his protection. Mum often talked of him to me years later when as she was recalling the past and she did so with much affection telling of his kindness, he had been such a gentle natured man and was always polite and a very giving man, befriending them all as he did, treating them with respect and understanding and he understood that Celia my Nanny had not been well with all the stress, he made sure that the family were made comfortable until they were due to set sail again. Sadly, they never did see Ashude again, but he stayed in their hearts and prayers always. They never knew if he survived the war, however, he has never been forgotten and Ashude would later become a Spiritual Guide to me in my mediumship journey.

When the transportation finally arrived to take them on to England it was not how they had imagined it to be. They found it to be a very large cargo ship called The Neuralia which had been gutted to accommodate the Gibraltarian families, Mum would say how they were loaded on like cattle and some were asked to go down into the hold. It was packed to capacity hot, humid and very cramped, they settled in best they could, and how in many ways it was a relief as they saw Africa disappearing into the far distance, and how they felt the sea breeze cooling things down, their journey now had begun, or as Mum would say, 'the nightmare began'.

Attempts were made by the British Government to make the ships habitable for the evacuee's journey, but the truth was, that they were in terrible conditions. There was little to no hygiene, no proper medical facilities and hardly any lifeboats or life jackets on board, certainly not enough for everyone. The ship sailed heavily laden into the unknown and the evacuees had much fear in their hearts as they knew the captain would have to try to avoid enemy U-boats that patrolled regularly in those waters. They did have an escort ship, which Mum thought to be French.

Of course, a lot of people were very seasick on the journey, Grandpop decided to move all the family up on deck, as the smell was getting unbearable below decks just after the third day. With the captain's permission, they made a small camp for themselves huddled together in one corner, trying to keep out of everyone's way at least the upper deck would be fresher and the air breathable they thought, pretty soon one by one other families joined them. The seas began to get rough, the drinking water was on ration, but the air was fresh and Nanny, who had been really ill on the second day of travelling, badly needed that fresh air. babies were born that had to be delivered by the evacuees themselves. It was to be a very long scary 17-day journey of hell. My Nanny and Mum would tell me stories of this time in their lives when I was young, as it had stuck with them as some sort of nightmare and has stuck in my mind ever since. They told of the night they were torpedoed, just at the halfway stage of their journey. They had been so very frightened and it was a miracle that they all survived, if it had been a direct hit, many lives would have been lost, as the ship was packed to capacity.

The upper decks now became overcrowded and the smells were still unbearable with so many people being ill. Provisions on board were also low, my Nanny recalled it was one of the worst times of her life, but she would also add that they were so lucky and grateful to be alive. She was a strong Catholic lady my Nanny and her faith carried her through, I'm sure.

Finally, they docked on the 17th day and discovered they were at a place called the Liverpool Docks. Many of them are ill and some are just exhausted, dehydrated and hungry. Slowly, one by one they disembarked they were weak and tired and had to find their land legs again, but they only had a short journey to their accommodation which was very close to the docks, but they were soon to discover they were in a worse situation than they had been in Gibraltar. The Liverpool Docks at that time were being constantly bombed by the German Luftwaffe. It was called the "Liverpool Blitz" as they sustained heavy bombing night after night. Reports of these bombing raids were not widely reported and kept very low key, as not to inform the Germans just how much damage they were actually inflicting on our docks. My family with many other Gibraltarian's had been placed right in the middle of it.

After many weeks waiting anxiously for news of what was going to happen to them, Grandpop, along with many of the other Gibraltarian families, got some information out of the authorities and they were to be loaded onto special coaches and, much to their relief, taken to another destination. However, when the time came to leave and they had boarded the coaches the driver told them he was heading for London. They were so relieved to get out of Liverpool, but little did they know what hell was ahead of them yet again.

On Arriving in London Nanny told me how they were all shocked seeing the large grey buildings with many bomb damaged, sitting in mounds of rubble piled up just like a battle ground, when the coach eventually stopped outside their accommodation, they found themselves in Gower Street, London. Yes, right slap bang in the middle of the city and yes once again they would be bombarded with bombs each day and night. The air raids were constant, people were fighting fires and many running for their lives, every evening my family lived in terror. Grandpop knew he had to get them all out and quickly.

It was even more terrifying, when they could hear the Doodlebugs buzz overhead and then that terrible silence, not knowing where they would be falling but it was usually somewhere very close. The buildings were crumbling around them with people constantly running for the Underground shelters as the sirens filled their hearts with fear, sleep was near to impossible, if they fell asleep it would be out of exhaustion. Mum had said she was very frightened, but at least they were all together and so far, all still alive.

The Underground stations would be packed with service men and women as well as local families and whilst the raids were on, people would laugh and sing and try to keep their spirits up. Groups would sleep huddled together to keep warm, top to tail in some cases for the children. My family were once more in great peril in The London blitz.

By now the Xerri family had been separated from many of the other Gibraltarian families that had come over with them. Grandpop made enquiries to sort something out himself or he feared they would all die in a bombing raid, there were too many close calls and they were not getting any information through to help their situation from the authorities, he managed to contact a good personal friend who lived in Hertfordshire explaining to him of their predicament it was to his great relief, that his friend offered them a house to rent. It would only have three bedrooms he had told them but it was situated in the countryside, a small village called Bushey in Hertfordshire. Their prayers had been answered, gathering up their few belongings they left immediately, it would only take a couple of hours by road to get from London to Bushey in those days' circumstances being difficult at that time but the arrangements were made and they fled from London.

Imagine the feeling of elation when the family finally arrived in the quaint little village of Bushey, the bus dropped them off in the High Street, the driver gave them directions to Clapgate Road. It was a short walk downhill from the main village, not that they had very much to carry as luggage. It was calm, almost heaven, in those peaceful surroundings and the sky was clear. The air is fresh at last, no smoke, no dust to fill their lungs, no smell of death.

3
My Dad

My Dad, Bill as a young boy when he joined the army

My Dad was James William Stanners but everyone called him Bill, born to Sarah and George Stanners on the 23rd March 1918 the youngest child of seventeen children, they lived in North Shields, Newcastle. He always said later in life that the beaches at Tynemouth were the most beautiful he had ever seen in the World and he was well travelled during the war. In those days growing up in that area was a hard existence for him. He had joined the army saying he was a year older, as many did, being enlisted around 1935 at the age of seventeen. Starting out at the Woolwich SE18 training camp of the 1st Training Brigade, RA Barracks, known as 851180 Gunner Stanners 1/24/35, as part of the Royal

Artillery. He would not have been allowed in the army if he had given them his true age, but he always said he knew deep down, he needed to get a better life and learn a trade, and the army was his opportunity to serve his country which he loved. Newcastle at that particular time was going through a tough time, as there was a lot of unemployment and coming out of school early as he did, he found himself getting into all sorts of trouble. He had little education but a lot of common sense and his mum, Sarah encouraged him to get away, to better himself as she knew that it would indeed open doors for him.

Sarah, my grandmother whom my dad adored, was a strong loving woman, she baked her own bread and worked hard all her life, she was to pass with breast cancer quite early, her husband George Stanners was never talked about much by my dad. I think George was an early passing also and I suppose when you have 17 children it was tough. George did not have a lot of time for any of the children. I feel there was not a lot of love there between my father and him, but maybe I am doing George, my grandfather, an injustice. Dad only spoke of his beloved mother, Sarah, and her kindness and a sister Bella who he was also close to.

Dad had been in the army for about four years learning a trade when at the young age of twenty-one he was sent to Gibraltar for special training and it was there, he met a young Gibraltarian girl. She had just turned 15-year-old a vivacious looking girl with black shiny hair and tanned skin, big brown eyes and an amazing smile, his description, always. She worked at the ice cream emporium at the corner of Pitman's Alley where she lived. She was called Maruja Xerri my Mum. Dad was painfully shy and bought a lot of ice cream as an excuse to see her. When he did finally pluck up courage to ask her out, she informed him that he had to talk to her father for permission first, and my Grandpop, took to Bill immediately and the date was arranged, 'walking out' as they called it.

Like a scene from *The Godfather*, the couple would take long walks, whilst following behind were many family members, keeping an eye on them. He was a young handsome man and she was young and very innocent, they fell deeply in love instantly, Bill asked her to marry him without hesitation very soon after they met, Nanny and Grandpop gave their permission for them to be engaged, but on the understanding, they would wait until the war was over to marry. Dad was a young Richard Burton look-alike handsome and strong; he had trained to be a paratrooper, a Red Beret. Much later in life after the war he was never one to parade and show his medals off, but we also learnt after he died, he was part of the SAS regiment. He had done a lot of training in Rabat as part of the parachute unit, the Red Berets. He was in fact an unsung hero; he was sworn to secrecy about it and took his secrets to his grave. By chance we found a tiny bit of paper in a box with all his army details and we were speechless when we discovered his military past, we were all amazed when that information came to light, he was indeed SAS and went on special missions.

Army photo of my Dad in his early 20s

So, my parents, young and very much in love, had to go their separate ways as Mary was about to be evacuated to England as you know, whilst Bill's war had just begun. As part of the 2nd Battalion Parachute Regiment, 1st Brigade, the 1st Airborne Division he left Gibraltar and was dropped behind enemy lines into Italy and it was in February 1943, he was eventually captured in action. Dad was first taken to Capua Transit Camp 66 near Naples in Italy. Later he was transported to Germany where he would be a prisoner of war for over three long hard years. POW number 258583. Whilst being transported from Italy to Germany by rail my father actually saw Hitler, he along with other men and women were all packed in cattle wagons like animals. He had managed to get to the side of the wooden wagon and there, through a gap in the wood which he had used for a little fresh air, he actually saw Hitler on the platform. He called him a few names, I am sure, and he was amazed how short he was in stature. For over three and a half years my father was ill-treated and malnourished in a prisoner of war camp there in Germany, until eventually he was liberated by the Americans at the end of the war.

Dad returned to England and made his way to Bushey to see the love of his life. Mum hardly recognised him, as he was gaunt and so painfully thin and she found he was not in the best of health. He looked dreadful, the Germans had kept him in a terrible condition with only rotten potatoes and what they called black bread and rotten turnips to eat. He had also suffered a nasty rifle butt injury to the back of his head, which made one of his pupils in his eye permanently damaged. He had said the Italian camp was bad, but at least they shaved his head to rid him of the head lice, but the German camps were hell on earth.

My father, Bill was such a very brave man. I am sure he could have written a book himself, but he would never talk of his experiences unless it was within the company of a direct family member, having a conversation with a few pints down the local pub and even then, his conversations were guarded. He would soon change the subject, as you could tell the memories were too painful and, in many cases, shocking, and with some memories being too hard to recall, it was still there etched on his face. The pride I have for him in my heart is immense.

In April 1945 the war was finally over, it was said Adolf Hitler committed suicide by swallowing a cyanide capsules and some reports say he shot himself in the head, in fact there are many versions of this demise that have been told, some say he fled to Argentina with Mengele and other Nazis. These evil men should have been brought to justice, as they would have a lot to answer for with their inhumane acts but I am sure they would have to face up to how they lived in Spirit world, that I do know.

In England one by one the men returned from war, the Germans had now surrendered and VE day was on the 8th May 1945 which was one hell of a celebration. Japan also surrendered later in the September of that year, after the horrendous bombing of Hiroshima and Nagasaki.

We all now know the full horror of what an atomic bomb can do, how it obliterates and kills not only human life, but nature, and our mother earth, with its long-lasting consequences to our planet. Surely this has to be one of the hardest lessons learnt by man and I pray it will never be repeated.

We will and should never forget the atrocities of that terrible time. The Japanese and German prison camps were liberated, and at last we were bringing our men home. Camps such as the one in Auschwitz with its gas chambers and crematoria, brings forward in our minds just how inhuman and out of control things got. These events in our history should never be forgotten if lessons are *to be learnt. The people who suffered in all these camps should never be erased from our minds. There are countries all over the world still in conflict. It saddens me at times to feel we have learnt nothing.

4
Bushey

The Xerri family must have looked very strange to the village folk of Bushey. These eight bedraggled evacuees walked down the hill with only a bag or suitcase each. Looking ragged and exhausted, although all probably talking ten to the dozen in Gibraltarian with excitement. Exhausted and ready to finally get into their new home which was situated at the bottom of the hill in Clapgate Road on their left. It was a semi-detached house with a very large bay window, Mum told me it had been such a welcome sight. Nanny and Pops swung open the brightly painted yellow wooden gate and walked along the tiny path, finding the keys to the house under a large stone, two large concrete steps led to the front door which was also painted yellow with a side window to the right. There was an amazing passion flower plant with its purple and gold flowers spreading around the door frame. Nanny had told me later in my life that this passion flower was so special to her as it had once been used to teach children about the history of Jesus.

> *The ten petals symbolised Jesus's 10 faithful apostles*
> *The Five Anthers represent the five holy wounds Jesus suffered*
> *The circle of fibres in the centre of the flower represents The Crown of Thorns*
> *The three purple marks represent the three nails*

What a lovely story to tell me, her granddaughter, I thought at the time.

To be finally in a place they could call home was wonderful, Nanny walked into a good-sized hallway, she told me how the house seemed to greet them, she felt comfortable straight away, and as it was south facing the sun shone straight through from the front door to the back. Everyone darted in all different directions dropping their bags at the door looking in all the rooms and running up the stairs to find where they would sleep. Their home in Gibraltar 12, Pitmans Alley, had not been very large for all eight of them, but as they were in the centre of Gib and just off Main Street, they loved the hustle and bustle of everyday life there.

Nanny and Grandpop's

However, this new home for them was very welcoming, spacious and more importantly it had a feeling of safety and warmth, with a peace about it. There were two large rooms downstairs and a small kitchen and a good-sized garden which had two small separate lawns and a path running down the middle, leading to growing areas one had fruit trees which were laden with Victoria plums and apples and to the other side was a large vegetable patch ready for harvesting: fresh food at last. Outside the back door there was a square concrete area and grandpop inspected the coal house and the outside toilet as most people had outdoor toilets in those days.

Upstairs the two bedrooms were reasonably sized, but one was called a box room being so tiny. Nanny and Grandpop had the front bedroom with the large bay window for themselves, and all four girls shared the other large room whilst the lads shared the box room between them. There was a wash room with a bath but no inside toilet, they would be a little cramped, but it was peaceful and it was safe. Away from the bombs that had rained down on them every night since they left their home in Gibraltar, finally they all felt secure in their new home in England, and I know my nanny would have said her prayers of thanks.

Bushey village at that time was calm and so different to London, everyone knew everyone else. There was a great variety of shops, Stan the butcher with sandy hair, who always had a friendly smile for everyone, Mr. Palmer owned the hardware shop he also supplied paraffin for the lamps and heaters, and bags of wood kindling for the open fires. Mavis's shop sold curtains, dress material, wool and sewing cottons, a tiny flower shop was a pleasure to walk past with many home grown flowers being sold the fragrances would be wafting out at you as you walked past. A small chemist and pharmacy was situated at the centre of the High Street and on entering that chemist shop you would see a large plastic deep sea diver holding out a net so people could return all your old medicine bottles for recycling. The fish shop had large marble counters packed with ice with fresh fish everyday laid on the ice, their mouths open and eyes staring. Favourite shop with the children was the toy and bike shop which was run by a Mr. Jordon and just opposite a large post office opposite, there were various tiny antique shops and a selection of good English pubs of course. Such a variety, everyone talking to each other, in normal village life. Grandpop's heart would leap when he heard a horse trotting along the roadside delivering milk or coal, giving him memories of his past life; they were in a perfect English village.

Once settled in their new home they would see and hear the planes go over each night heading for the city of London, my Grandpop would apparently sit on the back kitchen step swearing at the German planes in Spanish, but this time his family were not the target. It was said Bushey did in fact have a bomb drop and it landed in a place called the Moatfield, thankfully no one was killed, as far as I am aware.

Mum & Dad on their wedding day

Some of the local villagers gave my family a bit of a tough time at first, but it was understandable, it was war time and I guess these total strangers with tanned skins and speaking very little English stood out. For some it was fear of the unknown I suppose, but word soon got round the small community that they were proud Gibraltarian's, "British you know" Nanny would say.

As they got to know their neighbours they won over the hearts of the villagers, as once they knew why the family had been evacuated and realised what they had given up for our troops, things got much easier. Nanny was a hard-working woman, but also had a great sense of fun and good humour, my mother and her sisters got jobs working in the local laundry by day and by night they volunteered to do fire watching, their two brothers later joined the armed forces. Over time the whole family actually became very loved and accepted by the locals in Bushey.

There were always regular local dances which were a special treat as all four girls Mary, Vera Vicky and Violet would go together, Grandpop's rule. The sisters all had long black hair and tanned olive skin, they loved the attention they got from the local lads, dancing gave them back some fun in their lives doing the swing as they called it and the jitterbug. Mum had sent regular letters and food parcels to Bill, sadly only the odd letter got through. She would ask the local girls in the laundry how to spell certain words when adding a letter in the parcel, and dad would receive a letter from her saying she was working very hard in the laundry and how she was in charge of all the SHITS (sheets) girls will have their fun.

When the war was over, my parents were finally reunited, the whole family said how shocked they were to see Dad, on his home-coming after the war was over as he had not only lost a lot of weight, but he was not the same strong young twenty-one-year-old they remembered, Nanny was determined to feed him up and restore him back to health before the wedding and all the family rallied round. Dad took Mum back to Newcastle, to meet Sarah, his mother as George had passed to spirit by then and the two-woman got on really well. My parents were married in the Bushey Congregational Church and my dad managed to get a job on a building site for a while as there was not much work for all the soldiers who had returned from war at that time, they had to take what they could.

Dad had done engineering in the Paras, but to make a little money he found work not only on building sites but he also did a stint as a fireman and was a casual labourer. Dad and Mum lived at Clapgate Road with the family after they were married and in 1946 Mum fell pregnant. She had a really rough pregnancy and a very tough home-birth. If it was not for Dr Young, the local GP of the day, sitting with her through the night giving her sips of brandy, she may not have come through it, it was a touch and go situation, my sister was eventually delivered weighing in at over eight pounds. It was in mid-July Mum sent Dad to get her birth registered, he had strict instructions to call her Linda but Dad had other ideas. When he returned with the birth certificate it read Maruja Stanners.

It was 1947, things were moving slowly. Grandpop's and Nanny had given Dad and Mum the tiny box room for themselves, but it was not ideal the house was already crowded and now with a small baby and Mum still in recovery after the difficult birth things got harder Dad was struggling trying to adjust after his terrible experiences in the POW camp and it was decided between them, to get a place of their own. Things were very tight money wise, but Dad found two rooms at an affordable rent just off Bushey High Street, however, Mum had always said to me that these were difficult times for her as she found herself being stuck there alone all day in two tiny rooms with a demanding baby girl, whilst dad was out at work all day, she found the dark long winter days were setting in, and so was her depression.

Mum actually missed the family home and all the fuss and bustle that went with it. The two rooms in the flat were small and dark and she felt isolated, the walls became slightly damp in patches and when it rained, mould patches formed on the walls, there were no sea views, no sunshine, no garden and the long dull wet rainy winter days took their toll on her health. She soon became more depressed and anxious and also became withdrawn. Mum lost a lot of weight during this time and would not go out much without Dad being by her side. Her English was all self-taught and quite good by then, although she did have problems with her spelling still, Dad soon realised how anxious she was becoming and decided to get her out of the rooms and started looking for another place to live.

He got to hear about a small attached cottage which was empty and for rent. The landlords were the owners of the King Stag Public House in Bournhall Road, Bushey, a pub which still stands there today. Grandpop's and Nanny lived just two roads away and the rent was very reasonable, so Dad and Mum went for it, and they got it.

The cottage address was 19 Bournhall Road, Bushey. I can still see it in my mind's eye as childhood memories. The tiny gate, then a small path which led to the blue painted front door, to one side a raised patch of lawn overlooked by a large sash window and by the front door an old tree stump to one side, around which Dad had put a heavy chain to attach to the pram in case it rolled into the road. On entering the cottage, you would walk straight into the front room it was tiny but square, the three-piece suit and coffee table would be in front of the small tiled open fire with a large radiogram in one corner of the room and a glass China cabinet to the other side, two wooden cupboards housed the gas meter with slots for coins.

Left: Vera with me as a baby
Centre: Vera with me on her lap and my sister at S.G. Browns Christmas Party
Right: My aunty Vera and Michael, a special Bro, and me with hair at last. Sadly, I have no baby photos with my Mum and Dad at all

As you walked through you would take a step down into what we would call the back room. Again it had another tiled open fireplace and you were greeted with a dining table with four chairs. Mum had a small treadle sewing machine given to her which she put in one corner, there was just enough room for a small sideboard. The back window overlooked the garden but the light would be blocked out if someone opened the large wooden latch door to the staircase, which was very steep with high steps. They led to two small bedrooms so there was no landing as such. The small kitchen was at the rear, with a back door leading to a small yard into the garden. This was a big bonus as Mum once again could sit in the sunshine, which she loved and would watch my sister and I play. As luck would have it, the cottage was in a sunny position. Here was an outside toilet in the yard - complete with a big hairy spider.

Over the first three years in that cottage sadly, Mum's acrophobia and nerves got the better of her and it was to get much worse. She would never go anywhere without Dad, even a trip to her parents' home was an effort. She felt confined to the cottage, but at least the small garden would allow a little reprieve from the inside confinement. I suppose she felt safe in the cottage but this horrible medical condition was to last for eleven years, maybe it had something to do with all the bombs raining down on her from an early age, and she needed a safe place. There was no counselling for stress in those days. Three years went by and Mum fell pregnant again for the second time. This birth was much easier and I was born on the 12th November 1951, her second daughter. However, Mary's illness had taken hold and she was just unable to cope with me. Vera, her eldest sister, seeing Mum in such a bad way, stepped in without hesitation to help and it was decided that I would go and live with her until my Mum was better. I was a very demanding baby covered in eczema sores. I was a fright to look at with very unsightly scars all over my body which would weep and become infected. I had no hair on my head, just these large unsightly scabs, like the worst cradle cap ever. All my joints were filled with these cracks and sores. Behind my ears and in the fold of my elbows and knees, the skin would bleed if rubbed - not exactly a pretty baby at all. I didn't have any photos as a baby, in fact none until I was about six or seven months old.

Vera was my angel on earth, offering to look after me, and definitely a life line for my Mum. I was to stay with my Aunty Vera from birth for the first three and a half years of my life, making regular visits to my family home as my Aunty Vera made sure that the contact was always there. She already had a son called Michael and he would be my big brother for that short time of my life and I can only remember snippets of events. Michael was to sadly pass in a tragic road accident in 1970 aged just 21. Vera and Bunny, her husband also went on to have a beautiful daughter called Carmen who I keep in touch with and a son called Brian who sadly passed to Spirit 2nd March 2018.

When my eczema got worse Vera would bath me in milk and wrap my hands in bandages every night so I didn't scratch. If the sores got really bad, they would crack and bleed and itch, also if I got too warm or too cold, they would hurt and she sat up night after night to comfort me through some really difficult nights. She was my second mum and her husband, Bunny, was wonderful to me, they lived, in a small prefab at that time but I have very few memories of that, I just know I was well loved, I always held Vera and Bunny close to my heart and I was so grateful for what she did for me and my Mum, I am so glad I got the opportunity to talk to her years later in my thirties when I had a family of my own and she came to stay with me from her home in Adelaide Australia.

I was nearly four when Vera and Bunny took me back home to live permanently. She told me it was such a difficult thing for her to do as both of them had bonded with me and treated me as one of their own.

My Mum was in a much better place and more able to cope when Vera eventually took me back to live at home again, I was delighted to have my Sister around as Maruja was nearly eight by now and we would play well together always, when Vera had taken me for visits, it was our bonding time and I guess Maruja was ready to have her little sister back full time, Maruja and I became very close immediately, it had been my Sister that named me as when I was born, and she was very protective of me. My sister had spent a lot of time with my Nanny and Grandpop when she was younger and at last, we were reunited and ready to be a proper family once more.

Dad managed to get himself a position in an engineering company in North Watford called S.G. Browns as a precision engineer finally being given the opportunity to use his skills from the army. However, soon after starting his new job and just as things started to improve, he became very ill, he could not keep food down and was losing a lot of weight. Hospital tests showed he had massive ulcers in his stomach and he had to have a major operation. In fact, the surgery was to remove three quarters of his stomach, this was due to the fact he had eaten rotten food for over three years in the prison camps. The procedure went well and after the operation he was sent to Deal in Kent, an army convalescent home where he would remain for just over two months to recover fully. He also suffered from post-traumatic stress PTSD, Post Traumatic Stress Disorder from all the trauma and experiences of the war, but in those days, it was not fully recognised and the men that came home with this condition had to cope as best they could, when he was hit on the head with a rifle butt, it had left him with an unsteady nerve. He never talked about it much, but was embarrassed, when his head would lightly shake sometimes for no reason, usually when he got stressed, but I think only he really noticed it more than other people.

Vera returned from Australia to see me once more, around 1984

Dad could have a slight temper after the war but soon mellowed, he never raised a hand to Mum or us girls. His nature after the war was to be a bit of a loner, not enjoying crowds or too much company or any loud noise. A good man through and through. He loved peace and quiet and getting out in the garden, he would always be on hand to help others, and he was afraid of nothing. As children he was our hero, in so many ways, when a large spider would appear in our bedroom, he always put it outside gently cupping it in his hands saying they were good things as they ate all the flies, he was always very kind to animals.

Mum always had a strong faith. She was brought up a Catholic in Gibraltar although since being in England her attendance in church had ceased partly due to her illness. She was first and foremost a spiritualist and although she was not a medium herself, she believed in spirit world totally. She would regularly write to a very famous spiritualist called Harry Edwards who was well known as a healer at that time, he would send her absent healing and words of encouragement for her condition in personal letters all handwritten. It would give her a great deal of comfort, to receive these personal letters back from Harry, he would help her through her troubled times, later, as he got more and more well known, they would become typed letters but personally signed, Mum would send the odd postal order to say thank you and cover postage, but was never asked for money or donations. Harry Edwards was running a spiritualist sanctuary in Surrey and it's still there to this day. He was a very kind loving man, it's just a shame Mum never got to meet him personally.

I always played well as a child with my big sister Maruja, we bonded again easily. I was never a strong child, having eczema was bad enough but I also began to get asthma attacks which remained with me up to the age of about 10. If I laughed too much I would start to cough and wheeze or a simple cold would turn into a chest infection, that would turn into another breathing attack, my chest would just tighten, it was very frightening my Dad would ask me to breath into a brown paper bag whenever these attacks happened, this use to work as he was the calm one and it would prevent me from getting progressively worse. Mum, bless her would go into panic mode and with her anxiety I would then stress more. One year when I was still at infant school, it got so bad my bed had to be placed in the lounge so Mum could keep a constant eye on me day and night. I had a lot of time off school, months in fact the whole winter and was probably borderline pneumonia, the wheezing must have been unbearable for Mum and Dad to listen to, each breath was an effort. The snow that winter was about three feet deep and I can remember thinking I was missing out on all the fun. The winters in the 50s were very bad and there was a lot of green fog like thick pea soup in those days. Neighbours would pop comics through the letter box for me and sweets. The front door was never opened to keep in the warmth of the open coal fire in, and the cold air out. Mum would sleep with me each night until I was better.

My sister, Maruja, was a carer and helper to Mum in so many ways and she also watched out for me and at the tender age of 9 she would take me by the hand and go into Watford on the bus to buy my school shoes. Such a responsibility for one so young, looking after a five-year-old. She is, to this day, a best friend, sister and confidant. Our Mum relied on us so much, we understood that she was unwell and could see how painfully thin she was. When Dad was in the convalescence home my sister and I certainly stepped up.

In our front garden at the cottage. Maruja aged 9 and me aged 5

Our beloved Grandpop fell ill. Nanny was frantic with worry, as he had to have an operation on his heart for a faulty valve, I was only 5 but remember him well, sadly he did not survive, passing to Spirit actually on the operating table, leaving the family completely devastated, he was very much the head of the family and everyone's rock. It was January 1956, he was just 60 years old. These days doctors would have popped in a stent, or performed a routine operation to correct the problem, but they did not have that technology then.

Left to right - Nanny, Mum, myself and Maruja in the cottage garden, Dad took the photo

I have fond memories of my grandpop. He would visit my Mum at the cottage most days, sitting in the same chair by the front door. Mum would have a hot drink of milky coffee waiting for him, her specialty. He was always very smart wearing a brown pinstripe suit and wore a brown trilby hat and in the band of the hat he kept a white feather, he would take it out balance it on the top of his nose and then go into a wonderful game of pretending to sneeze, I would be in fits of giggles and delight. He was a wonderful man, so kind and gentle and loving, he could be firm and give guidance to us when needed, but always with that special wink. I don't remember the exact time I last saw him; I only have certain memories which pop into my mind which make me so happy. I never got the chance to tell him how much I loved him, but I guess he knew as my arms were always open wide to greet him and ready for those special cuddles.

However, when I became a spiritualist myself, I realised, we all get the chance to pass on our thoughts to people who have died, the memories of him greeting me with arms stretched out for that massive hug, makes me smile even to this day and how as a family we would all get together at the house in Clapgate Road, sometimes it was always a battle to get a word in, with everyone talking quite loud and all at once.

Nanny always said she would never remarry and she never did but went on to live alone at Clapgate Road for the rest of her life. She was a very vivacious, beautiful lady, slim in build with tanned skin, She loved the hot summers. Her eyes were the most amazing green, Irish eyes actually as her maiden name was Byrne. There would be a flash of anger in them at times and then you would see them warm and loving and full of laughter. I called her Abuelita which is Spanish for grandma or just Nanny. She would go to visit Mum most days, the pair of them sitting with a cup of tea and chatting in Gibraltarian to keep the language going, much of which I understood at that age. Nanny (Abuelita) would cook for the whole family at large family get-togethers, she loved everyone being there at the same time, she was the main spider in the web who would keep hold of the reins of the family unit holding them tight. There were arguments and squabbles but she knew exactly what she was doing. She was wonderful with people and would usually make them laugh and forget their problems lifting everyone's spirits. As a good catholic woman, she had a picture of Jesus above her bed and a bible on her bedside table and of course her rosary beads. She loved and lived for her family and was quite a character.

After Grandpop died, Nanny Celia started to smoke quite heavily, it was, I think, because it helped her to steady her nerves as she then had to cope with things on her own without him beside her. My sister and I loved her dearly, we admired her strength of character. She was amazing and everything she did, she did in style. She would usually wear an apron and tuck her cigarettes in the front pocket together with some mint humbugs, so she was ready to pop a mint into her mouth after a cigarette was finished. I can never remember her smelling of smoke, like some smokers do, I do remember her having a clean soap smell. Mum, Nanny, my sister and I were always very close.

She was in her element when all the grandchildren were there. Usually in the summer holidays, she would give us all a pair of tiny scissors and ask us to cut the lawn in the back garden as it would keep us amused for hours. When we complained about a blister, she would stick a plaster on our fingers and send us back to do more cutting. Her faith was strong and I feel that's what kept her going.

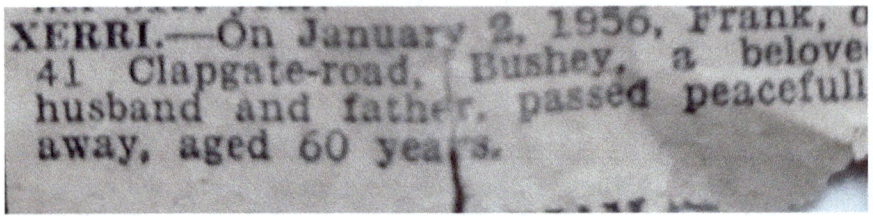

Grandpop's death notice in the local paper

5
My Sister, Maruja

Maruja and I have been through many difficult times together. The bond we had as children has never broken as she would always be there for me. I found it difficult to sleep when I first returned home from Vera's but my sister would place her hand through the side bars of my cot bed to hold my hand to comfort me each night until I fell asleep. I guess she has been doing it ever since, the memory is very vivid to me. I expect at that time I missed Vera and Michael and Bunny, but sharing the front bedroom in the cottage with my sister was a great comfort to me in those early days. I was her little sis and she was going to look after me.

The cottage where we lived in Bournehall Road, Bushey was, for me as a child, a magical place, especially when the coal fires were lit on a cold winter's night. Both rooms downstairs glowed with warmth, it was so cosy. We had a large velvet curtain which was drawn across the front room door. Being in a sort of burnt orange colour, it was so very warm and welcoming. No television in those early days, just a large radiogram with music always flooding through the house. Mum would pump up the volume in the daytime and turn it down quite low when Dad got home, him not being a lover of a loud noise, and I expect as children we made enough noise anyway. The Christmases were so special, Mum and Dad lit the fires in all the rooms including our front bedroom and they would hang Christmas stockings at each end of the fireplace. The winters were really cold with lots of snow as I remember, ice would form on the insides of the sash windows. Mum had been given a large fur coat by Nanny's cousin, Violet Pepper, a lady who worked in London for a Jewish family, I visited her there just once with Nanny, we loved Violet Pepper, she was such a kind lady and usually she would pop a half crown into our hands saying 'don't tell your Nanny'. She had a severe hunch in her back, after an accident as a child when she took a tumble down some stairs whilst carrying a heavy iron at the time. She made regular visits to Clapgate Road for her holidays and special occasions, we were her only family from Gibraltar who kept in touch. Her gift of that fur coat was heaven sent as Mum would place it on either mine or my sister's bed each night for an extra duvet for warmth, and Dad's old army coat kept us snug.

Bath time in those days (early 1950s) was quite a military operation in itself, a large tin bath was always hanging on a hook in the backyard just by the back door and it was brought in once a week and placed in front of the back-room fire. Maruja usually insisted on the first dip, being quite a lady and if we were lucky the water came up to our elbows. Such a chore for Mum to fill and dad would empty it when he came home, but we took it all for granted of course as kids you do, it was such hard heavy work for Mum and as I was a bit of a tom boy usually I needed more scrubbing as I was caked in mud from the garden most days.

In most gardens people had large concrete coal bunkers, ours was constantly being filled, because of the three fires that were our only source of heating so they had to be kept going. Mum's first job of the day was to take the ashes out and prepare the fires for the evenings. Once made-up and lit she would hold a large sheet of old newspaper in front of the fireplace to draw the fire up, then the magic would begin, but if she could not get the fire started because the wood or the coals got wet, you guessed it, we were cold and shivering until Dad came home. Every week we would purchase a small bag of kindling wood and a box of firelighters from Mr. Palmer's hardware shop in the High Street. This helped the fires catch alight quicker but when money was tight a rolled-up newspaper did the job.

Everything was recycled in those days, all cold meats such as ham, spam and corn beef were sliced straight off the machine and wrapped in paper. Carrier bags were made of brown paper with string handles. There were no disposable nappies, they were just soft cotton towelling, secured with very large safety pins, that would become rags eventually being used for washing the car or cleaning the windows. Milk was delivered in recycled glass bottles and pubs gave you a penny back on any returned beer bottles. Every garden in those days had a vegetable patch and a compost heap. I get a bit miffed when younger people lecture me on recycling. My generation was not a throw away society, we used everything after the war as things were greatly valued. My clothes were rarely new, as they had usually been passed down the line. The old clothes were kept until the rag and bone man came along with his horse and cart; everything went to recycle.

We didn't even have a hair dryer, and we let it dry naturally. Mum got us ready for a party one day as I remember and she was concerned that my long hair was still very damp, so in her wisdom she got out the hover and reversed it thinking it would dry my curls, I was instantly covered in thick dust and dad's fag ends Nice!!! We did laugh.

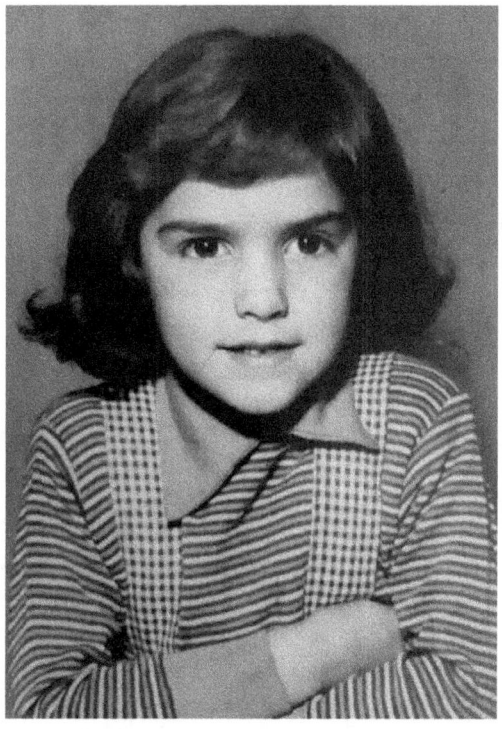

My school photo, aged 6

When having the coal delivered the coal men wore protective black clothing, their hats had large flaps over their necks their jackets had extending large shoulder pads, as these coal bags were extremely heavy being ordered by the hundredweight and these had to be carried round in to the back gardens and loaded into people's coal bunkers. If a delivery was due and we were home, Mum would ask us to check the number of sacks coming in and when the coal-men left, she would give us kids each a bucket each so we could retrace the their steps searching for any bits of coal that may have dropped off the load whilst bringing them in. It was surprising how much we would bring back following the trail sometimes to the bottom of our road. The coal fires were our only form of heating except for a paraffin heater in the outside toilet keeping the giant spider that lurked in the corner warm. When it got really cold Mum and Dad had a paraffin heater in their bedroom for warmth.

They had inherited an immersion heater that was installed in the kitchen but Mum would say it was too expensive to run. We had a meter for all energy and Mum would have to pop shillings in to keep things going. When she had no money and there were times when we lived from one week to the next, she found a farthing fitted and did the job. When it came to the meter being read and emptied, instead of a rebate Mum would get her farthings back, bless her. With only dad's wage coming in things were extremely tight.

I was not particularly that clean as a kid, especially after coming in from my playtime outside in the street, we would often go to bed having done face, hands and teeth. This was all done at the kitchen sink. Maruja and I would usually be sent to bed at the same time. I can remember always saying my prayers in my head and being out like a light. The King Stag Pub next door was not usually too noisy, in the week, occasionally Maruja and I would sneak into our parents' bedroom as from their back window we could look into the back room of the pub and we would watch the men playing darts and snooker drinking their pints.

They were tough years for Mum and Dad financially, but Dad would always come home with an enormous Christmas tree, every year God know where he got it from, it was always fresh with roots, he would replant it in a bucket and we decorated it with bright coloured glass trinkets and there was always a large plastic star on top which we got from Woolworths, bright paper-chain decorations hung across the ceiling all handmade by us each year with balloons in each corner. Magic. Treats were a lemonade shady with our Christmas dinner, a large chicken was cooked by Mum and she made a special garlic stuffing and they were truly wonderful Christmas celebrations. Maruja and I were given each a doll in a crib for our present. Maruja called hers Julie and I named mine Rodney for some reason. Mum had made us these cots out of oval plywood tomato boxes, and she had hand stitched the baby blankets and pillows which were just beautiful so unique, just out of odd scraps of material. What a special gift. The dolls had knitted outfits all handmade by Mum and wow, not a computer in sight. She must have worked on them each evening after we went to bed as they were a complete surprise.

My sister and I both went to Merry Hill school in Bushey Heath, it is a school steeped in history that can be traced back to 1827, a large red brick building with high iron railings outside which has not changed to this day and is still running as a successful school, with a mixture of the old and new buildings now. What I did not like were the very high windows, I expect they were designed to stop children like me gazing out and losing concentration.

Merry Hill school, Bushey Heath

Dinner times were my dread, the teachers would always quote to us "they are starving in China" and make us eat everything on our plates. I would sit and cry, being force fed large green tinned peas which I hated, or something equally as horrid, I loved my Mum's Mediterranean cooking of grilled fish and pasta, all the Gibraltarian dishes she had as a child were my perfect menu, my Mum was never big on roast dinners or meat and two veg. My sister Maruja, being four years older, became a table monitor at school and would collect my plate when the teachers were not looking, squashing the uneaten peas and other equally horrid food between the plates, then walking off in a hurry clearing them before she was caught. If she had been caught it would have meant the cane for sure. I can't eat tinned peas to this day. You should never force children to eat something, they will eat it when they are ready.

Before eating we would have to sing before a meal:

Thank you for the world so sweet,
Thank you for the food we eat,
Thank you for the birds that sing,
Thank you, God, for everything

But I would add…

not the peas!!!!!!

Merry Hill was a very good school but many of the teachers were very strict, I struggled a lot having missed so much through illness and was massively behind in everything, and in my last year I was placed with eleven other girls into a "catch up" class. My reading and general school work was dismal. This "catch up" class being so small helped so much and the teacher made us feel, not inadequate, but capable. She created a family, she made us realise learning could be fun and therefore we wanted to learn. The other classes would be green with envy as she would march us out of school on field trips such as fishing trips down by the canal in Watford. She gave us confidence and in that small class, I learnt more with the love she gave, than in my whole time at that school. Her name was Mrs. Walton, she lived at that time in the Cassio Park area of Watford, I know because she took us to her home one day for afternoon tea as an outing from school and a treat. God knows I loved that teacher. She brought out everyone's potential in that class. Dyslexia was not recognised in those days, but I had that also, all words were a complete jumble to me, and a lot of the other teachers just treated me like I was rather dim, but Mrs. Walton was such a wonderful person, my confidence grew with her. She even encouraged me to take part in the end of term school play. The other teachers were amazed that I had done so well and said that they had not realised I had that potential in me; it was Mrs. Walton's faith in me that took me forward.

My spiritualism was within me at that tender age, if anyone was unwell at Merry Hill school, the teachers would send for me and ask me to sit with them by the hand basins in the cloakroom, I would lay my hands on their foreheads and ask Jesus to heal them, don't ask me why it was natural thing to do for me, a dear teacher called Mrs. Judd, would call me "little nurse Stanners", I was at Merry Hill from the age of five until I went to secondary school at eleven. My favourite time was when the bell rang and we could go out to play, if I'm honest. As a child I never felt alone as there was always a presence around me.

Spiritual Knowings

Maruja, Jo and I in the 1950s

I had a very vivid imagination, seeing weird things sometimes and accepting it as part of life. playing at home I would have an imaginary lead and at the end of the lead I could clearly see a large Alsatian type dog. I did not give him a name but just knew he was with me and I knew when things got difficult, I was never alone. I never saw him inside our house, only when I would go out and about playing, he always remained with me. Later I was to learn that these are Totem Guides, he is still with me today. This dog (Totem Guide) gave me protection, loyalty, friendship and devotion and pure joy. Did my friends think I had lost the plot; no, they were too busy galloping around the playground on their imaginary horses.

Bournehall Road, Bushey where we lived as children, was always a busy road, due to The Kings Stag pub and there was also a bank at the top of the road, bringing a lot of parked cars around, which was great fun when we were all playing hide and seek; no drink driving as a rule in those days either, in fact we had very few problems with drunks coming out of the pub, as I remember, it was a much gentler way of life.

Maruja, Jo and I, today

Maruja and I would play out in the streets till quite late especially in the long school summer holidays that seemed to stretch forever. Our very best friend and constant companion in those days was called Josephine. She lived just two doors up from us on the other side of the pub, there was usually a gang of children about, but we three were like the musketeers.

We knew all our neighbour's and usually there was always a parent out gardening or cleaning their cars to keep an eye out for us. I was never allowed to cross the road unless Maruja took me across, very frustrating as I remember it. We would play "whip", a chase game like hide and seek but once you were found you would have to run like mad to get back to the whipping post and shout "whip!" before the seeker got there, it was great fun, all three of us would sit on a wall next to the whip post next to the pub entrance watching the world go by, Jo and Maruja would place their hands under my arms and literally hoist me up to sit in between them, years later when I revisited as an adult that wall was still there and so very low no more than three feet high. We were always close friends with Josephine, my sister being the eldest, then Jo and then me. She was our third sister and to this day we are still close.

Those lovely long school summer holidays seemed to go on forever, six weeks of sheer joy. On a Friday we would get pocket money from Dad, usually a florin, or half a crown if he was flush, my sister and I would go straight up to the High Street sweet shop as in those days as you could get loads of sweets, flying saucers, black jack's, sherbet dabs, knickerbocker glories, wonderful sweets, probably full of E numbers and the black jacks were dental filling removers for sure. Quite often we would wait at the top of the road to spot Dad coming home along the High Street on his push bike, he would stop and give us a ride on the crossbar back down to the cottage, I would ring the bell all the way and love it.

All the kids would sit in the big orchard at the top of Bournehall Road, it was a good hideout area although flats were built on the land later. One highlight of our week in the holidays was when the King Stag pub next door had the beer barrels delivered. We would watch the men pull back the two large cellar doors at the front of the pub and on a warm summer's day the smell of the hops wafting up out of the cellar was lovely. Usually, two men would roll the barrels down on ropes into the cellar, the lorry being parked up on the path. The delivery men also wore heavy leather aprons with thick black leather pads for their shoulders and thick gloves, if not the ropes would have burnt their hands as they lowered the heavy barrels one by one into the cellar. We kids would count them in and say hello to Mr. Lack the publican standing below waiting to receive the barrels.

Many times Mr. Lack would pop out with a lemonade or a packet of crisps for us, all free, just as a treat for such a dear man. We would sit on the steps after the lorry had gone, eating the crisps and last to go was the little blue bag containing the salt that was washed down with Tizer or Lemonade was yum.

Jo's mum, Jean, was such a lovely lady, in fact she would become one of Mum's best friends at that time, she knew of Mum's problem with her agoraphobia so would pop in most mornings and collect a list if Mum needed any shopping done in the village, they would have a good chat, making each other laugh about the local Bournehall Road news. and on Jean's return Mum would have ready for her a special cappuccino milky coffee, which Jean enjoyed. Jean was a shy lady and would blush at some of the things Mum would say to make her laugh. Mum said many times

Jean was her special angel on earth. They were good for each other and had a lot of affection for one another. Jean had the most amazing eyes: she was a beautiful woman with a ruddy complexion that of a real country girl, Jean had three children and Jo was her middle child she was married to Les who worked locally, the family moved away eventually purchasing their own house in Bushey, but my mum always talked about Jean with so much affection and love, I often think of Jean myself, as she was so kind to me.

I would often play in the front garden of the cottage on my own. Mum would leave the front door wide open which meant she could see me even if she was in the kitchen, and she always made sure the small swing gate was firmly closed. Mum knew if anyone passed by, I would start talking to them. I was a right little chatterbox.

An elderly gentleman would walk by in the afternoons after lunch usually at the same time every day on his way to the pub. He would meet up with his pals and put the world to rights, he told me, he had a medium sized sandy coloured dog with him which had a wiry coat such as a lovely gentle natured dog called, Ginger. This dog would be eager to see me and stick his nose through the gate to get it tickled, the old gentleman always stopped and chatted asking me how my day had gone. I liked him very much and would usually ask Mum for a biscuit so I could have it ready for Ginger as a treat. All adults to me in those days were Uncles and Aunties, so I called him Uncle Ben. Mum sometimes would pass the time of day with him and there was a calm about him and a very gentle nature, he was very well spoken and when Mum would appear at the front door, he would lift his hat when saying hello to her. I looked forward to these encounters especially in the school holidays, Maruja being older would play with other friends at times. So, for me seeing Uncle Ben was definitely a highlight of my day, I would have loved a dog and Ginger fitted the bill.

Days went by and with no sign of Uncle Ben, I would sit on the front door step and eventually eat the biscuit myself. Was Uncle Ben, ok? I would ask my Mum repeatedly; you know how persistent children are. I would get quite upset and eventually after all my nagging Mum decided to enquire at the pub as to how he was. The pub landlord told her that Uncle Ben was very unwell. Without hesitation I decided to send him a letter and in my best handwriting, I wrote a small note wishing him well and telling him how I missed our chats and Ginger. To my amazement I got a reply, which was one of the most beautiful letters I have ever been sent. Sadly, I never saw Uncle Ben or Ginger again, but he has never been forgotten by me, he has guided me since his passing, I am sure. I sense him or he just pops into my mind and always I get cold legs, that's a sign to me there is a spirit dog about, maybe Uncle Ben is still walking Ginger in spirit word.

I reflect on those days with affection and the thought of Uncle Ben. He always gave me the time of day, asked my opinion on things and made me feel so special, it's so important for a child to be listen to, instead of being talked at, his letter, which I have kept over sixty years, is in a special box still gives me upliftment when I am feeling low. People sometimes are sent to us to give us guidance and help, they may be people we may not know well, but they do uplift us in many ways.

I will never forget this man.

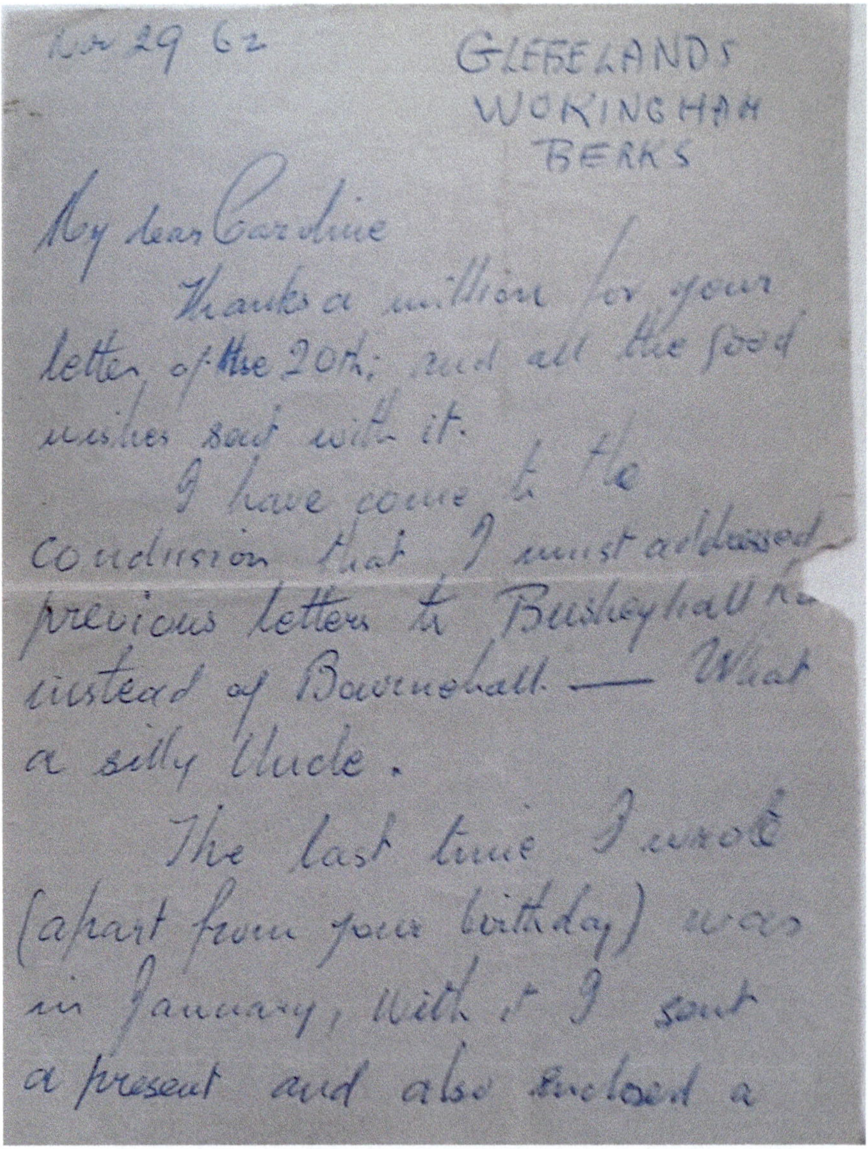

> Nov 29 62
>
> GLEBELANDS
> WOKINGHAM
> BERKS
>
> My dear Caroline
>
> Thanks a million for your letter of the 20th; and all the good wishes said with it.
>
> I have come to the conclusion that I must addressed previous letters to Busheyhall Rd instead of Bournehall. — What a silly Uncle.
>
> The last time I wrote (apart from your birthday) was in January. With it I sent a present and also enclosed a

Page 1 of Uncle Ben's letter

a short note for Maruja
and a present for her also
———— Your letter was in
rhyme ———— it went something like this

"To day I am feeling FINE
So I'll write a line to CAROLINE.
And thank her for her well-written letter
The contents made me feel better.
The writing is so neat and clear
Keep it always like that my dear.
I'm glad your 'Flu' has flown away
And does not return for many a day.
MARUJA'S modeling excites me also.
She has good form and shapely TORSO.
The BIRDS are singing songs of SPRING.
Soon the FLOWERS we'll be GATHERING.
Your MOTHERS letter was a special TREAT
I'll answer it when next we MEET."
THANKS FOR YOUR LOVE AND PRAYERS DIVINE. GOD LISTENS
———— And TO LITTLE GIRLS LIKE CAROLINE.
you never received
it. I'm so very very sorry

Page 2 of Uncle Ben's letter

> Do write again soon and say you forgive me for being so stupid.
> I did promise to come and see you but it was not to be. My condition and bad weather would not allow.
> I am still looking forward to seeing you, dear, <u>it may be anytime now</u>
>
> God bless you all
> Love
> from
> Uncle Ben
>
> My wife thanks you and sends her love

Page 3 of Uncle Ben's letter

Still confined to the cottage with her illness Mum never ventured out further than the garden and on rare occasions we all went to Nanny's for tea, but only if Dad took her. It made me think a lot about those times during the Covid lockdown of ours, and how she must have felt. I never want to portray my Mum as a dull, ill person, she was full of fun and laughed a lot, she had a great sense of humour, there was always a good happy atmosphere in that cottage. Friends and family were always welcome, she loved my father dearly and we two girls were her life. Maruja and I were carers in many ways, going to the local shops and delivering lists for food deliveries. I think they must have been very lonely days for mum in many respects. She was painfully thin, but never lost her beauty, people just loved her gentleness. She ate very little, maybe grilled fish and buttered crackers and drank weak black tea. She could have only weighed about 6 stone: in those days her face was beautiful but a little gaunt at times.

There was a car-lot in Bushey High Street, just at the top of Bournhall Road so in an attempt to get mum out and about my dad purchased a car on weekly payments, he had his eye on a black Ford Anglia, with two large bright orange indicators like ears at each side and too enormous silver chrome headlights at the front. The interior would smell wonderful as it had real leather seats. Maruja and I were so excited and would help Dad wash and polish it every Sunday, putting Duraglit on the chrome. Then he would take us for a spin, it was good to see Mum out and about, but it was usually after much persuasion from Dad and we didn't go far as soon as she was out with us. She wanted to go back home at first, but it gradually got a little easier.

Mum was very protective of us girls, yet she would send us on missions, doing the shopping at really young ages, usually on our own, armed with cash and a list. If I was asked to buy ham and came home with it too fatty, she would send me back with a note asking that the ham be changed and it would be changed. In Gibraltar you helped your parents and grandparents by doing chores, in many ways we grew up quicker with the many extra responsibilities we had did not seem a burden. We would prepare meals and dust and hoover, do washing and hang it out, my sister and I did the ironing and always made our own beds, we would walk to school on our own or with friends from the age of five. In Gibraltar everyone knew everyone else it was really safe growing up for Mum, and I suppose as Bushey was a small community Mum felt it was safe for us, but she would depend on us more and more. When I was just about 8-year-old Mum asked me to catch the bus to West Watford and visit the engineering factory where Dad worked, he was off sick and his wages needed to be collected, as the rent was due, I had to get two buses in fact it was a miracle I didn't get lost, I remember having strict instructions to zip the wages up into my pocket for safety. When I got back, she asked what had taken me so long!!!

In the 50s a lot of shopping was done via the door-to-door salesmen. They would call to the house every week with large heavy suitcases full of anything and everything. They were called tally men in those days. Everything would be paid for by weekly payments and as the clothing coupons were being phased out it was a great idea for people who were on a tight budget. Mum did not have much money to play with so it was ideal for her especially as she was unable to go out to the shops at that time, with her illness. We only had Dad's wage coming in, although Mum made pegs at home. A gross of pegs would bring her in a little extra cash, she also made Christmas crackers in November. It was like a production line, we all helped in the evening listening to the radio. Her pay was very poor, as you not only had to make them but also box them up.

My sister and I at the S.G. Browns Christmas parties in the 50s

Our tally man was called Mr. Silvero, always smiling, he was a regular caller to the cottage. He was not very tall but well-rounded, always dressed in an immaculate grey shiny suit, he had thick black wavy, slicked back hair with the Brylcreem look, a very ruddy complexion and a rather large red pitted nose on which he perched his large black framed glasses, which he would constantly push up to prevent them sliding down, he wore many gold bracelets and chains and had heavy gold rings, his aftershave knocked you back when he entered the cottage front room, but an ideal salesman, he could talk for England and was very likeable.

In his large suitcase Mr. Silvero would have an array of delights such as dresses, shorts and tops, underwear, socks and school uniforms for us children. We would always wear Sunday best, white socks with sandals, clean dresses and cardigans, with large bows in our hair. I don't recall Mum buying much for herself, but she would, as a treat, buy my sister and I, every year an amazing party dress each to wear at the S.G. Brown's children's Christmas party these dresses usually had puffed up underskirts, which transformed us into feeling like princesses. At these parties there was always a visit via a mini train to see Father Christmas and at the end of the firm's evening we would collect our presents. Aunty Vera would always step in to take us each year.

One month when Mr. Silvero was on holiday, a new salesman arrived at the door. He was a very tall slender looking Indian gentleman, immaculately dressed in a smart linen suit and he wore a large lime green turban. He looked amazing and was so very polite, Mum welcomed him in. He had a beautiful face and the most amazing blue eyes sparkling and yet deep and thoughtful, even as an adult now I remember him as he had such a gentle smile. His soft black beard was neatly shaped and he was very softly spoken, with teeth that were like white pearls and his hands as I remembered neatly manicured and slender.

Mum bought some bodices for us girls to keep us warm in the winter, so I suppose he was pleased to have made a sale and felt relaxed, so when Mum offered him a cup of tea, he accepted. He and I sat down on the sofa, whilst Mum made the tea. When she came back into the room, she started to tell him about her life in Gibraltar, I sat beside him and he reached across and cupped his hands around my face and told my Mum with a smile, that I had been here many times, this is just another journey for her he said, she is a very spiritual child. I felt very important and there was a magic about this man and I could not take my eyes off him. There was nothing uncomfortable about it or weird; he was kind and his eyes told me so. He made such an impact on me Mum thought he must have been a very spiritual man himself, and I felt that day, that he had looked deep down into my soul as I had looked back into his. Mum was delighted that he saw this in me and from that day forward, she would talk to me more about the spirit world and her beliefs.

Even at that very young tender age I was interested in God and faith, as Mum always said that saying prayers for people if they were poorly, was a good thing to do and there would always be someone listening. We were taught about the Bible and Jesus in school and Maruja and I also attended a group for children called *The Crusaders,* which taught us even more about the Bible. Although Mum was a Catholic, she never went to church, and Dad was church of England, the catholic faith did not recognise their union. This was a thorn in the side of our local catholic priest who would constantly come and knock on the door to tell Mum to attend church and to repent of her sins, she would not usually answer the door if mum saw him coming, and we would hide in the back room. On one occasion she opened the door and he stood there telling her that she was not married in the eyes of God and how it was a sin to of had daughters and actually used the B word, being unaware that my Dad was off work that day and sitting in the back room listening to every word, Mum tried to get rid of him but he was persistent, but for Dad enough was enough, he rushed from the back room and literally ran to the front door and went nose to nose with this priest and said if the priest ever came back he would knock him out. It didn't seem to upset Mum at all when she talked about it later in life, she just felt very sad that a priest could have been so unkind.

I would often walk down the road to see my Nanny as there was only one road to cross and the traffic in those days was not as bad and the engines seemed a lot louder, so you could not only see but hear if something was coming. We were taught in the 50s at a very early age *Stop Look and Listen,* look again, then and only then if nothing is coming walk don't run across the road, the local police often came into Merry Hill School with traffic awareness demonstrations, and road bike training. It does stay with you, my parents would always drum this into us girls when we left home, I looked forward to my visits to my Nanny as she always made me welcome, getting me a drink and something to eat, then we would sit in her large sunny front room and chat, everything in there was spotless large comfortable brown leather chairs with lace headrests and armrests stiffly starched and a piano along one wall which all the grandchildren wanted to play when we all got together. In the corner by the door was a tall table with a large black telephone on it and a dining chair at the side On many of my visits if I asked to play the piano as it was a big attraction for me but Nanny would say No Aunty Winnie next door has a headache, she had a lot of headaches when I wanted to play for some reason!!!

Winnie would often pop round no locked doors in those days she would just appear through the back door, calling "coo wee Mrs. Xerri it's me". I would sit and listen to them talk, Winnie had lost her lovely husband Charlie early to cancer and was in need of company at times and Nanny was in the same both having lost their husbands early, all the family had moved out of Clapgate Road by then, Mum's sisters were all married to Englishmen and her two brother's married English girls, that's why the family remained in England.

My Aunty Winnie as I remember was very glamorous, she worked in the local chemist in Bushey High Street and she always looked immaculate, with her tightly permed blond hair, red lippy and bright painted red nails, also she would smell wonderful with strong perfume wafting around her, the make-up she wore was always well applied, and she would never do housework without wearing rubber gloves as I remember. Winnie would always call my Nanny, Mrs. Xerri, and she was such a lady. The two women were so different but got on well together, always ready for a giggle and gossip to cheer themselves up, Nanny had a great sense of humour. Winnie had two children Michael, who had been Mum and Dad's page boy at their wedding, and a daughter called Maureen, who was the same age as my sister Maruja and they became good friends in their teens.

On one of my visits Aunty Winnie popped in and was telling us that she felt a little down and was thinking of going back to church every Sunday, but she was not sure what she believed in anymore since she had lost Charlie. She said she felt alone and empty and needed to get her faith back, it all kept pouring out of her till eventually there were tears. I knew my Nanny could relate to that as she listened and let Aunty Winnie pour out her feelings keeping a sympatric ear, Winnie was saying, she did not know how to get motivated and Sundays for her were such a long day, So I chirped up and said let's do a tour Aunty Winnie, every Sunday we can go to a different church in the village and see what we think. To my amazement she beamed and said, "Well, if it's ok with your mum I will pick you up every Sunday morning at nine thirty for ten o'clock service." And for the next three Sundays that's exactly what we did. Maybe she was glad of the company, it takes courage to go somewhere on your own for the first time, or maybe it was meant to be.

The Catholic Church, Bushey Village, Hertfordshire

Mum agreed straight away so there on the doorstep early that first Sunday morning, stood my Aunty Winnie in a very bright yellow cotton dress with matching hat, shoes and gloves in white, her hair neatly tucked away from her face, she looked wonderful, I was so glad my Mum had insisted on getting me dressed in my Sunday best, despite my protests at the time. My pink cotton dress was crisp and clean, my white ankle socks were new and I wore a pair of white sandals that Dad had used Blanco on the night before: I thought I too was very smart.

Spiritual Knowings

The Congregational Church, Bushey, Hertfordshire

Our first visit was to a new Catholic Church in the lower part of the village. It had not been there that long; it was a new building with an enormous statue of Jesus on the front and with very large stained-glass windows which reflected the light from all angles, quite beautifully. I did not expect it to be so modern. However, the service was very long and in my opinion as a young child of about seven or eight, boring, I was not impressed. Actually, I was rather glad when it finished. On the way home, I was wondering if my suggestion had been such a good idea. We had been greeted on the way in, but no one chatted to us much after the service, so we came away feeling a little flat. I could tell Aunty Winnie was not very impressed either, dropping me off at home, she thanked me and to my surprise said 'See you next week'.

St James Church in Bushey High Street was next on the agenda. I loved the look of this church, it was easy on the eye, parts dated back to the thirteenth century and in the 50s it had a large duck pond in front complete with ducks, an arched gateway led to the front entrance, the gravel pathway was lined by many very old gravestones. As we entered, we saw a carved wooden pulpit to one side, it had so much history I sensed it straight away. The service was long and the sound echoed around the church. I noticed we were again feeling complete outsiders. After the service had finished, Aunty Winnie told me it was a *high church*. I thought she was talking about the steeple. The atmosphere again was not a relaxed one and on the way home Aunty Winnie announced it was not for her either. She told me that the last port of call would be where my Mum and Dad got married - the Congregational Church, so that was our next target.

On that third Sunday off we went again. On arrival the church members welcomed us straight away at the door and during the service Aunty Winnie and I had a giggle-moment, when she crunched a polo mint and it sounded so very loud, as everyone was in silent prayer. I joined in the hymn and quite enjoyed it, as it was one, I sang it at school and was familiar to me, but I had no intentions of returning the following Sunday, I was all 'churched out'. We got back late that Sunday as Aunty Winnie had seen quite a few ladies she knew there. We did find, unlike the other churches; people came up and invited us for a coffee afterwards. As a child you know what it's like standing there with adults chatting, I think I did say 'are we going home soon'. The bonus was being given chocolate biscuits and orange juice. On the walk home, Aunty Winnie announced that she would be returning to the Congregational Church as she had seen a lot of old friends there that she knew and would be comfortable returning on her own, although, if I wanted to join her, I would be very welcome. To be honest, it was not for me, I was not impressed with any of them at that tender age. I guess I just had an inquisitive mind. My Aunty Winnie did continue to go back to the Congregational Church each Sunday Morning and she would go on to make new friends, giving herself a new interest and a reason to get up and out on an otherwise quite Sunday, so I guess it was all for a reason and it did her good. For me, my future Sunday mornings were back out playing in the garden, getting as muddy as possible.

I was very much a tom boy at that age, but loved to do concerts for Mum, singing and dancing in our small back garden at the cottage I would stand on top of the concrete coal bunker with castanets and a Spanish fan usually in Mum's old high heels, Mum would clap and sing, I loved it with my audience of one. I always had rather a lot of cuts and bruises to my knees and must have been a complete nightmare.

St James Church, Bushey, Hertfordshire

My delight was to run and play and get dirty, in our garden that was what I enjoyed most. We had two large concrete plant pots that stood at the entrance of the rear garden path and as kids we would make mud pies in them, Maruja would made leaf pancakes and we would also find garden snails to race when Jo came round, dobbing a bit of Mum's nail varnish on their shells to tell whose snail was the fastest. A large Cox's apple tree stood at the rear end of the garden and was usually laden with fruit and as kids we would go down with aprons on, holding them out wide whilst Dad would climb the tree give it a shake and it would rain apples, dropping them into our outspread aprons below, such happy days. What we didn't keep we shared with the neighbours.

My Sister was my best friend despite the four-year gap, we worked together well in the house or at play she watched out for me in most things, I know I could be very irritating as the younger siblings can be, we did argue, at times, she just wanted her own space but generally we got on well.

Mum would always have the radio on, filling the cottage with music from people like Perry Como, Matt Monro, Frank Sinatra. Dad loved Anne Shelton singing *Don't Fence Me In* and Mum loved a song called *Out of Town*, by Max Bygraves her favourite lines as I can remember her singing:

*"Up there the sun is a big yellow duster polishing the blue blue sky
with white fluffy clouds in a cluster hanging in the breeze to dry.
Trees everywhere with blossoms in their hair
and mother nature wears her sweetest gown."*

............wonderful.

I can still hear her singing it in my head, she actually had a great voice and the hit Green Door by Frankie Vaughan was a favourite as she had a crush on him. Programs like The Navy Lark and Jimmy Clitheroe were popular and Sunday listening was with Two-Way Family Favourites - a request program for families with loved ones in the armed forces, with Jean Metcalfe and Cliff Mitchelmore hosting it. We didn't get a television until I was about eleven, so in the early days the radio was a complete joy.

In the adjoining cottage to ours there lived a very elderly couple called Mr. and Mrs. Norris, I think they lived there because the cottages belonged to the brewery and the couple had run a pub for years, called the Cat and Fiddle. They intended to see out their retirement in Bournhall Road. Mrs. Norris was maybe then in her late eighties, Jack her husband, adored her. I called him Uncle Jack, we never saw Mrs. Norris much, as she was very frail and stayed indoors a lot, only occasionally would she sit in the garden with us for a smoke and a chat, when Uncle Jack would pop out on his push bike for shopping. Mum would pop next door occasionally just to make sure they were both ok and to ask if we were making too much noise for her, but I don't think they ever complained, the walls in those cottages were pretty thick and solid. I popped round a few times to say hello with Mum, but found her a little bit frightening at first, as she always dressed in black, like the Dickens character, Miss Havisham, as I remember her I can still picture her as being very pale and willowy, with a pointed face, she looked tired and sad at times and a rather large cat would sit on her lap, she always made me feel welcome and I made her smile, with my constant chat. Jack was not a tall man; he always wore a checked jacket and flat cap. He was very kind and had a gentle nature. They were private people but Uncle Jack would always go out of his way to say 'hello' to us children if he was in the garden.

One day we found Mum sitting in our back room with tears in her eyes, she explained that Uncle Jack had passed to Spirit world that morning and was wondering how Mrs. Norris would cope on her own without him. When my dad arrived home from work that winter's evening he went through his usual routine of taking his push bike down the garden path to lock it in the shed overnight, when he walked in the kitchen Mum blurted out 'Jacks died this morning Bill', dad looked visibly shaken and in shock. He sat down straight away and said he can't have, I've just seen him walk down the garden just now, I said 'Evening Jack and he nodded to me and doffed his cap'. Mum and Dad looked at each other in amazement. I guess this was my first bit of evidence that life went on after death, but they never spoke of it again. I remember going to bed that night thinking it's ok, we don't really die, we are still about. Mrs. Norris, bless her, was moved out almost immediately after Jack's passing. I think she went into a care home or with family and the cottage next door would stand empty until we left years later. Mum looked forward to some new neighbour's moving in but the pub who owned it never did rent it out again.

Sadly, Mr. and Mrs. Lack the landlords of The King Stag decided to retire and leave the pub and a new family took over. They were friendly enough and Mum and Dad seemed to get on well with them, until the bombshell hit - they wanted us to move out as they intended to knock down the cottages for a car park. This was Mum's worst nightmare. The pressure was on.

6
Bushey in the 50s

In the mid-50s Bushey High Street in Hertfordshire was a very vibrant place to live, with lots of tiny independent and individual shops. I had two favourites, one a large toy shop run by a Mr. Jordon and an antique shop, with weird and wonderful things in it, from furniture to old coins, and house clearance items. I would peruse all the odd bits of bric-a-brac and furniture and all the fascinating items of jewellery left on tables outside for all to view, lots of old coins and general odd and sods of curiosity, it was a real Aladdin's cave. When Dad gave us our pocket money one Friday; I decided not to spend it all on sweets and when passing the antique shop, I spotted on one of the outside tables a was small black leather Bible with gold edged pages that were wafer thin it fascinated me so much I asked the shop owner if I could purchase it with my pocket money, he agreed and for less than a shilling it was mine. When I got home my parent's looked at me with amazement. Dad said it must have belonged to someone very religious as it had writing in the borders. I can remember Mum saying, 'Well it's better for her than all those sweets, I still have it to this day, one of my treasured possessions albeit a little battered. I never did as a child attempt to read it; I just popped it under my pillow every night. It had maps in the back and a name *C Lee 15th Sept 1894*. Perhaps they would have been happy to know I looked after their Bible. The black leather was slightly padded with a little of the stuffing coming out, and over the years it's become quite tatty. I still love it. It looks very sorry for itself now. Perhaps one day I will get it restored.

I feel children today should be protected more as in the world we live in; on the internet they stumble on all manner of things that their young eyes should not see. I had none of this to contend with, and I often feel how wonderful it would be if the kids today could go out to play in the streets as I did as a young child, without their parents having fear in their hearts for their safety. We were of course told never to talk to strangers but in those days, things were so different, adults were not afraid to say hello and engage you in conversation and I guess we felt safe. After all it was a small village and we knew most of the faces that were about. people would say 'How's your Mum', or 'Give my love to your Nanny', that's what you get in a small community. People were just called Aunty or Uncle and always talked to us with total respect. I could never get to the end of the High Street without someone saying something or just giving you a smile. We respected our elders and had innocent fun, most of our food was home grown, fresh fish or meat and life was good even though we did not have much money at all, we all had each other, many of the adults' conversations were 'Thank God, we made it through the war', and it just made us realise it was good to be alive. In 1961 Uri Gagarin made a single orbit around the earth for the Soviet Union and the Space race began, exciting times I thought.

The King Stags landlords went ahead with their plans for the car park, they gave my parents just a little time to sort themselves out. I could see how anxious Mum was, she was actually starting to have panic attacks and she lost even more weight, bless her. Dad kept popping in to see the local council to explain the situation and as luck would have it, they had a council house allocated to us straight away and it was still in Bushey. My sister had just finished her secondary school education at Bushey Meads in Coldharbour Lane, and had got herself a job. I was eleven and due to start my time at Bushey Meads that September. I failed the eleven plus but then had to sit an exam to see what stream I would be in at the new school - they went from A to F streams. Amazingly I managed to get into Stream B. Thank you Mrs. Walton.

On the weekend Dad drove all of us to see our new council house. We had not got the key yet, but it was more to show Mum how close it was to Nanny's house and to stop Mum from fretting. The strange thing was we had been in that same road and parked outside that same house just the week before, when we took one of my school friends' rather large tortoises back, having looked after it while she was on holiday. She lived at the bottom of Chivette Close and the Close was opposite the house we had been allocated. As Mum and Dad sat waiting for me to come back up the close, Mum had said to Dad on that occasion 'I wish we could live in a house like that', the door was open and she could see into the hall and the kitchen, and she liked what she saw, unbeknown to her at that time, she was looking at her new house. Someone was listening. I like to think Spirit was listening.

A couple of weeks later it was ours, Mum fell in love with it: we had three bedrooms, an indoor bathroom with toilet, no more hairy spiders to contend with, one large hallway with a good-sized lounge, and the kitchen downstairs overlooked the garden. It was south facing so the sun would shine all day, bright and airy. A ten minute walk to Nanny Celia's house and the lounge window had a great open view of The Close opposite which was always busy with the comings and goings. It seemed to flick a switch in my mum, one of hope for better things.

The garden was much larger laid to lawn with a massive vegetables patch at the rear and Mum absolutely loved it. Electric heating with a gas fire in the lounge and for mum it would mean no more building fires either. The move took place during my summer holidays from school. It was a long hot summer. I was looking forward to starting my new school and our new life.

We had been in the new house in Pentland Road for a matter of weeks when we heard of an accident that happened back at the King Stag pub. It was around five o'clock in the evening when Mum would have been in the kitchen preparing Dad's meal with my sister and I helping, the large red brick chimney stack, which was very high and very heavy, was struck by lightning and fell into the cottage kitchen. Everything happens for a reason Mum said calmly. We would have been killed for sure.

I did miss the cottage dreadfully at first, with memories of sitting with my sister holding a long toasting fork in front of the open fire waiting for the freshly baked bread to turn golden brown. slapping on heaps of butter, wow. I would talk to Mum telling her exactly where my Dad was on his journey home from North Watford, as I could picture his journey in my mind "he has passed the shop, he is coming up the Avenue and finally just coming round the back now" I would say and the door would open as Dad would step into the kitchen. Mum always said to him, 'She has done it again Bill'. The pangs of missing the cottage would soon fade, but the memories as I get older are more vivid. The modern gas fire in our new home was lovely but it never did have the same appeal.

For me living in Pentland Road, Bushey things certainly did improve, my sister and I had our own bedrooms at last, which gave us that personal space we both needed. I was now getting on for twelve and she was sweet sixteen. I noticed we had rather good-looking neighbour's all lads, which was all new to me also, I had always thought boys were something to be avoided at all cost. I was still a bit of a tomboy at heart, my new friend Dorothy who lived round the corner became my good pal and we would walk Pepe her poodle and another dog Mitcy that I walked for an elderly lady, over the fields Dorothy and I were the best buddies in those days, and it was good to have a friend to walk to my new school with. My new school being mixed classes, made me soon realise boys weren't so bad after all.

Mum's three sisters, Vicky, Violet and Vera, took the decision to emigrate to Australia. You could do it for as little as ten pounds in those days, as long as you had a trade. They did ask Mum and Dad to go with them, but after much debate and soul-searching Mum and Dad decided not to go, dad loved England and they could not leave Nanny on her own and wanted to stay close to her especially since grandpop died, Mum's two brothers were still living locally and they would visit Nanny and Mum regularly. However, when all three girls left, it tore my Mum's heart out. She was devastated and would cry buckets, as Vera, Violet and Vicky her three sisters and her had gone through so much together and been so very close. They would, of course, correspond by regular airmail letters but for Mum it was never the same.

My dad got a new job working for Marconi Space and Defence in Stanmore as a security officer doing shift work. It was closer to home but the shift work meant doing long unsociable hours, he wore a uniform again and to be honest he loved it. My sister had a bit of money of her own now and was going out more and I was enjoying my first terms in my new school at Bushey Meads Comprehensive. For me it would be a struggle at times in the B stream, but my parents were so proud of me. I remember I did make a great effort to keep up with the homework. I was in B stream for all classes other than maths, I was placed in the C group for that and I always struggled to be honest, numbers jumbled as well as the letters. I sat next to Dorothy and two lads called Ray and John sat behind us, they became good friends to me and are still in touch with me to this day having reunited. When everyone had their hands up with the maths's answer I would turn round and give them a pleading look till one of them tipped me the answer.

Mum continued to write to her beloved Harry Edwards for advice, as his word always comforted her in so many ways, she had dipped slightly when her sisters emigrated and somehow Harry worked his magic to help her through it. He had told her to enjoy new beginnings and new challenges and not to be afraid of change, but above all to keep her spiritual faith solid.

Mum did start to get a new confidence about her and she gradually came out of her shell more and started to live a happier life. Our neighbours, Evelyn and Jim, became good friends, they also had two beautiful daughters who were much younger than us. Another couple called Nelly and Ernie, who lived two doors up, were wonderful people being so welcoming to my parents, their son and daughter were also good friends. Our immediate neighbours next door to our semi were Hilda and Tom. They had two sons just lovely neighbours - life was now good for my parents.

I feel I must say a bit more about Harry Edwards, he was to pass into Spirit in 1976, but the Spiritual Sanctuary that he founded is still there, it was established as a registered Charity in 1966, continuing his legacy and bringing healing to thousands all over the world. I know he gave so much comfort to Mum and many others, she always donated, when possible, just very small amounts as a thank you, in the form of a postal order, but did it without obligation or being asked to do so. Seeing how the foundation is still here today and people still getting so much comfort from it, makes me realise what a wonderful dream of his it must have been and what a wonderful legacy to have left behind, and it was all done in love.

Mum gradually put on weight and was so much better and we became a very happy family once more. Maruja and I still helped with the chores, because that's how we were brought up, but seeing Mum find her own space was wonderful, the garden to the rear was her joy to sit in. I might add she was not a gardener, it was Dad who started growing vegetables and he took pride in the lawn. Life looked bright and we were full of hope. Mum also started to venture out on her own and even got a job as a shop assistant in the local Bishop's store, which was a supermarket. Shop assistants were called the Bluebells, wearing light blue uniforms. Her dear friend Hilda from next door also worked at Bishops and sometimes they would walk into work together. Hilda would give Mum a lot of encouragement and confidence. I can honestly say everyone loved Mum there, she would make people laugh by talking to them in Gibraltarian. They nicknamed her Boo-boo. Mum began to flourish at last.

To my surprise one day Mum suggested a trip into Watford on the bus, just her and I. It was a day I will never forget, mother and daughter stuff, and a first for me. It had been great fun and whilst waiting for a bus to go back home, I spotted a bag in a shop window. Green tartan on one side and black patent leather on the other, I just admired it and before I knew it, we were inside and she bought it for me with her wages. We had never been kids to ask for anything, money was tight usually, but I suppose she was earning her own money now and wanted to treat me. I loved that bag, but loved the look on my mother's face more when she bought it for me.

7
Big School

In the 60s Bushey Meads Comprehensive School was a great school to be at. I was carefree and full of adventure but so much happened around that time. In 1962 we had the Cuban Missile Crisis, it was a terrible worry as for 35 days confrontation between the United States and the Soviet Union could have ended up as World War 3, it would have only taken one of them to have pressed the button. Also, in 1963 John F Kennedy was assassinated in Dallas, Texas, and Martin Luther King was also assassinated on the 4th April 1968 in Memphis Tennessee, followed by Robert Kennedy's assassination in the June of that year, these events sent shock waves reverberating around the world, and made me realise at that tender age how fragile life is.

As a young teenager, my head was full of things such as music, boyfriends, clothes and generally enjoying myself. Winning the World Cup in 1966 was great and celebrated by all. The World Wide Web did not arrive until 1991, so as teenagers we were in our own little worlds and had little interest in the news of the day. Unlike today where the news, good or bad, is in our face all the time, on social media and TV. Having to cope with mixed classes, as you can imagine, was not easy for me at first. It always led to romances and it was all quite new, exciting and fun. On all my reports it used to say 'Sensible but she needs to concentrate more in her lessons instead of gazing out of the windows', but the classrooms were so different, with large beautiful windows, letting the sunshine in, such a better energy for a school. The pips, as we called them, went off through the tannoy system each half hour to indicate that everyone had to move around to different classes. If your class was an hour long you could look to see your latest handsome crush walk past. It was the time of Motown Music, The Supremes, The Beatles, The Rolling Stones, the swinging 60s. The music was just great and you were a mod or a rocker, I wore lipstick and the darker your mascara and eye shadow, the better, the Dusty Springfield look. Skirts were high, very high and so were some of my friends. I never got into any of that and always listened to my parents 'wishes of respectful behaviour especially with boyfriends, my father was very strict, but in a loving way. In the fifties and sixties if you got into trouble, it was not easy for girls to keep their babies without family support. Playing records and listening to the radio especially on warm summer days was my idea of heaven especially if the Beach Boys were playing Good Vibrations… wow.

Me aged 15

Whilst at school I got a Saturday job in a local shop called Robertson's at the top of Clapgate Road, Bushey, Nanny had put me forward for it. Janet and Peter Nash who ran the shop treated me like family. In fact, when Janet had a daughter of her own, she called her Caroline, which I thought to be a great compliment. I am still close to Janet now, she's in her eighties and still has a wicked sense of humour. We chat on the phone about the old days. Peter passed to Spirit sadly, he was such a lovely, gentle and kind man and a great manager.

My Nanny would be a regular visitor to the shop and when standing in the queue, she would tell everyone 'She is my granddaughter you know'. I had many jobs there, cheese cutting, weighing and serving vegetables on the old-fashioned scales, filling shelves, packing at the checkout and eventually working on the tills myself, which I loved, as you could chat to everyone. I would pop in after school sometimes and make up the orders for customers, boxing them up ready for Nick the young lad who did all the deliveries, bless him he would be constantly teased by Janet, as he did blush a lot. He would go out on a heavy-duty black delivery bike in all weathers come rain or shine. I liked him a lot but he was very shy and I don't think we said much to each other at all.

My wages for all day Saturday were ten shilling at first which they soon increased to one pound with the evening work. These were to be some of the happiest days growing up. Janet made me a new cotton school dress in yellow strips when I became a prefect and a beautiful purple dress for the school disco and then took me to see the Sound of Music, just as a treat I think we cried through most of it, I love her to bits.

Bushey Meads was a very good comprehensive school; the buildings were very modern, with large playing fields and a large gymnasium which I loved. The school uniform colour was bottle green blazer white shirt or blouse with grey skirt or trousers very smart. I was able to wear that different yellow striped dress in my last year as I became a prefect. I used to fall in love every day, my head was in the clouds for most of the time talking about boys and music, mainly to my friends. Many of my old school friends have passed to Spirit and it saddens me as we never had mobiles in those days or Facebook to keep in touch. So, a lot of us simply drifted apart when we left school. The teachers were real characters and I do look back at that time with a lot of affection. I remained in the B stream until I left, but struggled dreadfully with maths in the C stream, usually I would get caught out by our Maths teacher, Mr. Locket, nicknamed Lucy Locket, he was a kind and gentle man, he would tease me for turning round to talk to Ray and John. Generally the teachers in those days didn't hold back. If you were late or forgot your PE kit, you got the 'slipper' and it was extremely painful. In class we would usually have to duck when the chalk flew through the air to wake someone up or get their attention. My lovely friend Sue and I generally sat next to each other, and would shudder when the teachers were in a bad mood. One teacher actually punched a lad in the stomach in front of the whole class; it makes me feel sick to think of it now. In that respect they were not the good old days, respect and discipline was always expected, but it should work both ways. In one of our gardening lessons, I was asked to pot up a bulb for the head master's desk. Instead I popped an onion bulb in the pot. I was summoned to the Headmaster's office and asked to stretch out my hand. I was given the hardest slap with a wooden ruler, tears rolled down my face, it was so painful. He was obviously not amused. I never told my parents because I knew my Dad would have gone into the school and knocked him out.

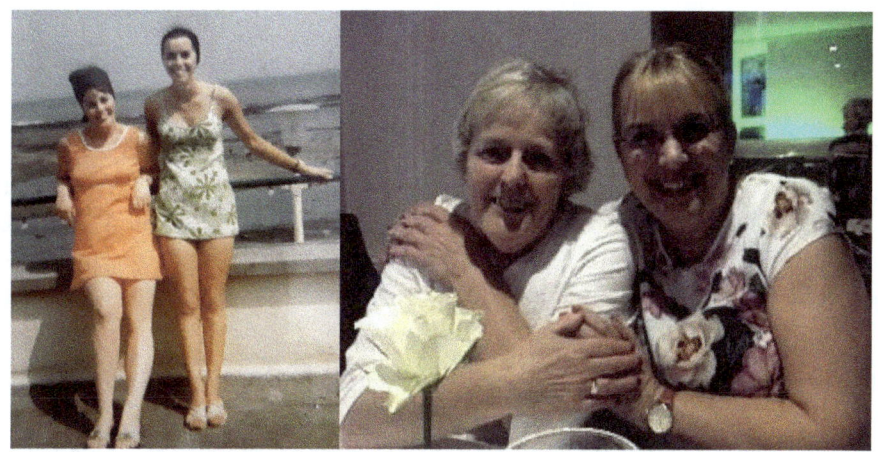

Left: Pauline and I on holiday in Scarborough
Right: Pauline and I in 2019

There was never any pressure from my parents for me to stay on at school: they were a little old fashioned and thought it would be best for me to go out and get a job straight away and to find a nice young man and get married. I do have certain regrets about this as I probably didn't find my full potential at school, who knows what another year may have done for me, perhaps changing my life's pattern. There were also so many special people there I would have loved to have kept in touch with. My friend Pauline was the exception to the rule as we were kindred spirits, we just clicked from day one and got on really well - still do. We became inseparable in my last year's and I would play hooky at times going to her house and listening to groups like The Small Faces, her parents took me on my first ever holiday to Scarborough and treated me like their own.

Pauline and I both left school in our fourth year, and both went for a job interview at Clements of Watford, one of the largest departmental stores in Watford. It was quite a grand and very old-fashioned store in many ways, with old fashioned values, everything was done in the old school traditions. Pauline went in for the first interview and I, being terrible at maths, was a bit unsure if I would succeed as I would be on the tills and dealing with money, when she came out, she said quietly 'He might ask you what an eighth of a pound is? It's two and six'. My interview went well but as I got up to leave his office, he stopped me and asked what my maths was like, 'Oh good', I assured him.

'So! if I was to ask you what an eighth of a pound is, would that be a problem'.

Two and six', I answered without hesitation. Thanks to Pauline I got the job.

Our friendship blossomed outside of school, Pauline and I were literally joined at the hip doing everything together, we just got on so well. Clements sent us both for further education to Cassio College in Watford for one day a week, she had been placed on the makeup counter at the entrance of the store and I was on the floor above in the fashion dept, and I started training to be an under buyer.

Every Thursday night we would go dancing at the local Top Rank and other girlfriends from Clements would join us. It was great fun and a magical time, wages were soon spent as soon as they were earned. My first wage packet contained four pounds, two shillings and sixpence. two pounds I gave to my Mum to keep. The rest was for bus fares and clothes, we worked nine am till six pm every day and on a Friday 10am till 8pm in the evening and all-day Saturday till 9 am till 6pm for less than a fiver a week.

Then Life changed.

One day I came home from work one day to find Mum crying on her own in the lounge. She told me she had found a lump in her left breast and after a hospital referral from the doctor's they wanted her in the next day for an exploratory operation. Mum was so frightened, bless her. The local doctor had been saying for years she had arthritis in her arm and that is why it ached so much, how could they have got it so wrong; she did not want to make a fuss and only discovered the lump when a delivery man at the store accidentally banged into her at work with a large plastic tray of bread.

My sister had changed jobs and was working at the local Peace Memorial Hospital in Watford, in the records department, dealing with doctors' clinics, where she met her future husband Roger, an ambulance driver. Mum said it was a comfort to know Maruja would be on hand and in the same building. The operation was to be done immediately, and Mum did not have any time to dwell on it, the next day when she was on the operating table the decision was made to completely remove her left breast to prevent the cancer from spreading, it was such a major operation in those days, but it was a lifesaving operation. I think I have blocked a lot of the pain out over the years as it was gut wrenching seeing this beautiful woman go through this. Mum was also in shock, as she did not have time to digest what had just happened to her, it was such a horrendous operation for any woman to go through. No reconstruction as there is today, no wonderful Macmillan nurses on hand to guide her through the trauma, just two extremely worried daughters and a husband in torment trying to cope with his stress over it. Mum was very brave especially as she had just lost a friend Megan to cancer with the same symptoms a few weeks before.

Through all these troubled times Mum never lost her faith in Spirit, continuing to write to Harry Edwards, getting strength and encouragement to fight the cancer. She did get stronger eventually, but then had to endure gruelling radium treatment in an NHS Cancer unit at Mount Vernon Hospital in Northwood. A lot of this she had to face on her own. She relied on us girls and close friends to talk to, but our Dad found it very difficult. He went into a shell, maybe he remembered how he had lost his own dear mother to breast cancer. It took Mum many months to get well, the radium treatment was far worse than the operation in some ways but she stuck with it. She did all the exercises they gave her as she had lost the ability to raise her arm, every day she would fingertip walk up the wall, we would try to help and encourage her to do this. Each day raising her arm a little higher each time, she was making some progress every day. Nearly half of her wardrobe was binned as she couldn't wear any low-cut dresses and none of her tops with cut away sleeves could be worn; in fact, nothing could be tight-fitting. All garments were to be cotton and loose, her skin was so delicate where it had been burnt by the radium treatment. The clothes options were not her style at all. It was devastating for her and she lost a lot of confidence, before this she had been a very voluptuous woman. We feared she would retreat back to her agoraphobia, but with the help of Spirit and the encouragement of her family and friends, she literally clawed her way forward and got better with true grit and determination. The first false breast they gave her was just padding, then she tried a gel one, but it was cold and heavy to wear and sore against her skin. In the end she would stitch padding into her own bra, which proved to be a comfortable solution. Remember this was over 50 years ago, we have made many advances since then in treatment and care.

To our astonishment she announced that she had got herself yet another little job, this time in the local newsagent, no heavy lifting just serving behind a counter, they were thrilled to have her and she told me she needed a reason to get out of the house. We were so proud of her. One of her sisters came back to England to live, the youngest Vicky, so it was nice for Mum to her to have back.

Mum was very popular with all the customers in that paper shop and it gave her a reason to bounce back, getting her life on track again. She would laugh and talk to the customers many she knew from working in Bishops. Life once again got into a routine, Dad still working shifts as a security officer was difficult for her as his shifts were staggered, some days he was working from 3pm until 11 at night, but she took that opportunity to have early nights and rest, my love life dipped drastically, and I was at an all-time low, so I would make sure I was at home to keep Mum company.

Dad loved his new job; he was always smartly turned out and had replaced his old car with something a little more modern - a bright yellow Ford Consul and things were again going well. I decided to get my driving licence as soon as possible and passed on my second attempt. My friend Pauline also got her licence and bought a car like the one in the Harry Potter films - a light blue Ford Anglia. I remember us going on holiday to Swanage in it and we shared the driving, such happy days. I would unofficially borrow dad's car whenever I got the opportunity, in other words when he was not about, as I could not afford a car of my own, one day Maruja wanted to go into Watford shopping and as Dad was nowhere to be seen I suggested I would drive her in, It was agreed I would drop her off at the bottom of Water Lane, in Watford and pop straight back home, however our plan went pear shaped as when we were approaching the bus stop in Watford to drop her off, she went into panic mode as she said Oh My God there's Dad at the bus stop, I slowed down she jumped out and had disappeared into the crowd. Then, as I edged my way forward to pass the bus stop the traffic lights went from red to green and there to my amazement was Dad, as the lights changed, I took off like a bat out of hell thinking I was in for it when he got home. Boy was I wrong, he came in laughing, saying you little b****r why didn't you pick me up? I am not cross that you gave your sister a lift, just cross you didn't give me a lift home. That was my dad.

Our lives as a family once again took an unexpected turn. Dad as usual took our small dog out for a walk in the evenings, when he was on early shifts. One particular night it was getting quite late and he had not returned. We all thought he might have stopped off at the local pub, but that would have been unusual as he was not a great drinker at all, but there was no better explanation. Then we heard the dog scratching at the front door and then a thud. Upon opening the door Dad staggered in, Mum's immediate reaction was to be cross, thinking he had indeed been drinking, he was all over the place. But we all quickly realised something was seriously wrong. He crawled up the stairs to bed with our help, complaining of a violent headache and was then violently sick. It continued through the night and finally at 2am that morning we called for an ambulance. Mum seemed to get strength from somewhere and took charge, even though she was still getting over her own operation, she knew Dad was gravely ill.

All three of us went in the ambulance, I sat behind Dad cupping his head in my hands as the roads were so bumpy, I remember the ambulance man saying to me 'That's right darling just hold your dad's head steady for me'. We all sat in silence in the waiting room then someone came out and told us to go home as they were going to run tests and we should return later the next day, although I don't think we got any sleep.

The following day we went back and on entering the ward we panicked and there was no sign of Dad, we were soon ushered into the ward office. All three of us sat stony faced and shaking as a young doctor came in with dad's notes in his hand and said don't panic your husband is in a side room, he could not bear the noise of the ward, and the diagnosis was a brain haemorrhage, we think the bleed is at the back of his head quite low down going into his neck, Dad was indeed gravely ill, we were just stunned. Mum said she always thought she would go first, especially with the cancer, my sister and I did what we could to comfort her, but we were all frantically worried.

Dad would be on open order at Watford Peace Memorial Hospital for three very long days and nights. We could stay with him all the time as they did not expect him to survive. Mum would be holding back her tears whilst with him, as we didn't know how much he was taking in about the situation. It was a terrible time, we were all in panic, first Mum then Dad, what else did fate have in store for us. I have never prayed so much asking for him to get better. The Watford Peace Memorial Hospital at that time was a very good hospital and the doctor told us that if Dad were to stand any chance of surviving, they would have to move him to the Whittington Hospital in Highgate, London for a major operation, but just the journey would be risky, however even if he did have the operation there might be the chance of permanent brain damaged. They needed Mum's signature for the go ahead with this operation, as time was now running out. As we sat in the office the doctor brought out several forms for Mum to sign. She had to give her permission for the procedure to go ahead, but to our amazement Mum refused, saying she needed to make a phone call first. Unbeknown to us she contacted the Harry Edwards team and the spiritual group, when she returned to the office, she came back confident and strong and had no hesitation in telling the doctors that from that conversation she refused permission for them to do the surgery, saying Spirit will take care of him and that the hospital needed to give him more rest and time to heal.

The surgeon surprised us all by saying he understood and they would give Dad another couple of days to rest, but against his better judgement and if there was no improvement, he would send him to Highgate for a second opinion. The three days went by with just a little improvement so another Xray was done and the doctors called us in for a consultation, this was crunch time, my heart was in my mouth as Dad showed no visible sign of improvement, the doctor told Mum 'Well my dear the valve that was leaking at the back of your husband's head is knitting together and healing', but I cannot give you an explanation for it, but the tests are clearly showing signs of improvement, his operation was to be put on hold for another week. Gaining a little strength Dad was eventually transferred to Whittington Hospital in London to have this confirmed by the top neurosurgical doctor, even though they had no explanation as to his survival. They could not explain how he had recovered, other than one doctor who said that it was indeed some sort of miracle.

The return to work for Dad was to be a slow one but over the next six months he was to make a full recovery. The doctors said the bleed was from an artery at the nape of his neck and that was where he had been struck by the rifle butt as a prisoner of war in Germany. The doctor said that was probably the cause and said it could have happened at any time. Mum was certain that spiritual healing had done its work, and so was I.

It just showed me at that time what a powerful belief my Mum had in the Spirit world and against all the odds she was prepared to put her trust in the spiritual healers. From that experience my own spiritual faith continued to grow and I know in my heart Spiritual healing may sometimes never be a complete cure, but it is there to help and should the person die it helps them with an easier transition, a miracle maybe, the power of prayer, definitely.

8
Watford in the 60s

Watford was the nearest large shopping centre to Bushey and my home town and place to go to for me in the sixties, it was where I worked and apart from lots of shops it had great cinemas, a large dance hall called Top Rank and a popular club called The New Penny, these were my favourites. Pauline and I would pop to Hemel Hempstead in her car if we wanted to go bowling, but in and around Watford there were lots of popular pubs to visit where young people would gather.

In Watford at that time there were lots of different opportunities to chop and change jobs taking you in different directions and in those days that's what a lot of people did, to be able to change direction was great for it gave folk like me an opportunity to seek what was right for them and you could work up to management skills and get an apprenticeship easily. I also worked for Salisbury's handbags at one time learning about different types of leather and then a shop called Stone Dry, which sold rainwear just opposite British Home Stores in the High Street, and it was at Stone Dry, I hooked up with Pauline again and we always had so much fun working there, actually managing the shop ourselves for a long time when the current manager left, until the head office decided to get a new full time manager in. I suppose we were very young for such responsibility but the shop was really making money when we ran it and ended up closing when we left. The decision to leave was a joint one as we both wanted to have our weekend free so office jobs were next on our agenda. Every job that came along gave us knowledge, in my opinion there is nothing wrong with chopping and changing jobs as it helped us learn about different things and life skills.

My home life was getting back on track with Mum and Dad in recovery and both back working, things were on the up again. Pauline found a job in a Laminate company in the accounts dept and as I was rubbish at maths I plumped for a job as an office junior in a Solicitors office called Arnold and Co, it was great as both jobs were within easy walking distance of Watford train station, enabling Pauline and I to meet up for lunch, and we also travelled to work together in her car.

Such happy days. Sometimes walking down a road together she and I would burst into a scene from singing in the rain, with our umbrella and splash in all the puddles, mad as a box of frogs. I felt very grown up working at the solicitors and on a couple of occasions I was asked to go up to London on the train and make my way to The Law Society in Chancery Lane, to collect some urgent forms. It meant catching a train from Watford to Euston then a bus to Holborn, this gave me a lot more confidence. My Boss was a real gentleman, very old school and I learned so much in that environment. The secretaries were kind and the receptionist I worked alongside called Carol became a good friend. It was very difficult for me at times, not being recognised as dyslexic. I had to do the filing and I would also read through loads of stuff with solicitors and secretaries checking wills etc. No one recognised my condition and I got away with it saying if we could do it slowly I would be more correct, they just helped me so much. Learning about Litigation, Criminal law and Matrimonial and Conveyancing, it was all very interesting. The confidence was building. I enjoyed the switchboard work immensely, I actually remember the first call I took on the switchboard it was from a firm of solicitors called Percy Short & Cuthbert so when I went to put the call through to the boss, I said 'Percy's shorts are on the line', and then began to go into fits of uncontrollable laughter about what I had just said, my boss just shouted 'PUT THEM THROUGH!!!!' - oh boy!

I had no desire to be a legal secretary, I knew it was not for me, as we had no spell checker in those days. I once had to type a one-page will for the same boss at a moment's notice as all the secretaries had gone home. The clients were due in the office within the hour. Being proud of my work I showed the people up into the office and presented the boss with the one page will I had just typed. At end of the will was a statement that went "If any man blah blah blah" a document such as a will has to be perfect with no alterations, so I felt so proud placing this document in his hands and hung around ready to witness their signatures but as he read it there was a sudden look of horror on his face and I saw the cigar tilt from his mouth, and he shouted I Fanny!! I Fanny!!!! (Not If Any.) It was corrected and initialled and I was dismissed for the day. My many mishaps, shall I say, were always forgiven by my Boss, as he always had that twinkle in his eye and was a good man.

I was fit as a flea, working there constantly running up and down three flights of stairs. but I knew I did not want to stay there for long as the wages, to be honest, were not great for the long hours, luncheon vouchers did not buy disco clothes, the bonus was having Saturdays off. Pauline heard of two other office jobs going in a large building called Star House in Clarendon Road, Watford. It was a Building Merchants called Pratts & Standard Range and we both thought it would be a complete change for us once again and the bonus of working together would make it perfect. The interviews went well, we both sailed through and were both placed in a large office side by side, on one of two large customer service desks, with six people on each. It was so very different as there were several floors to this building and lots of young people buzzing around, we had both been in smaller environments so it took a little getting used to. The manager sat on our bank of tables keeping an eye on Pauline and I and the other chaps and the desk opposite mine was empty as the chap was on holiday for two weeks, when he came back, I found it belonged to a John Rollo. I vaguely remembered him from school as he had been in the year above me, we all got on very well at work and he would always be eager to help me if I had a problem. Curiously, Pauline had spoken to him a few times on the phone when she worked at the laminates company.

The work was more problem solving and telephone work, more common sense really, I enjoyed it very much. I was asked later that year to be their Personality Girl alongside one other girl, it was to promote one of their new showrooms in Norwich, they took us up by car for the opening of a new depot. This would be my first time away from home on my own, staying overnight but I wasn't bothered, my faith had returned and I knew Spirit were helping look after me, Mum and Dad were very chuffed.

John was always teasing me at work and I remember thinking he was rather full of himself. and a little arrogant, then out of the blue in the lift one day, going up to the second floor he asked me out. "Where do you live?" he asked and when I told him he said he was not sure where that was. My reply, if you want to take me out you will have to find out - who was being arrogant now, I thought.

I had the green eye in those days, jealousy is not a good trait, the office was full of young girls all looking fabulous. If John gave them attention, I would give him the evil eye. The romance was very intense and we actually got engaged after a matter of months Rod Stewart's Maggie May and Marvin Gaye's, I Heard It Through the Grapevine were being played constantly, Mary Quant clothes were my favourite outfits to buy, and on some dates, I wore high platform boots and hot pants thinking I was the bees' knees. We went for a Chinese meal, John was very quiet through the meal and when he took me home, he asked me to marry him this was quite soon after we met, I accepted straight away without hesitation it just felt right, but I also made the decision to leave the job I loved as I felt it was the only way it would work for both of us by having different interests from one another. I was very young and too young to get engaged really, but that's how it was back then.

My head was completely wrapped up in him and everything in my life changed. Pauline was wonderful and our friendship remained strong, although we did drift apart for a while. Jobs were plentiful, I got another one straight away at a photographic shop in Queens Road, Watford. They needed a receptionist and after being there a while they asked me to do extra work by taking the wedding photo proofs to the various receptions in the evenings and get orders for albums from the families. An old A35 car which belonged to one of the boss's wives would be made available for me to borrow just for these events, no sat nav in those days, so I was constantly getting lost and I found it quite a lonely job too. I would also do the odd modelling job for them and ended up in the local newspaper a few times, my claim to fame, I wore a beautiful Rembrandt coat as I remember.

One day to my horror the A35 was not available and my boss gave me his spanking brand-new car to go off and do a job near Ruislip lido, I had been there once before but as he waggled the keys at me and said its parked round the corner, my heart was in my mouth. Mirror, seat belt, indicator, I looked back over my shoulder and indicated before pulling out, a man in a car behind impatiently waved me out of my parking space, so I gently pulled out only to have another inpatient driver behind him overtake him and as a result he smacked into the side of me, oh boy. If that was not enough, I completely panicked and reversed immediately, only to run over a parked bicycle. I just got out of the car and ran back to the office in floods of tears, they were wonderful about it saying as long as I was ok that's all that mattered. They said they would see the car and find the bicycle owner and I was to go home and not to worry. They never spoke of it again. I remained their receptionist for another year, but eventually decided that it was not the job for me.

9
Life for Me in the 70s

John and I going to a friend's wedding

I had seen a job advertised in Bushey Heath doing cold calling sales work. This would allow me to be near home and save more money for our wedding and I could actually walk to work up through the Bushey Recreational grounds, the walk was a pleasant one seeing the dog walkers and walking over grass surrounded by trees straight through to Highland Drive a road which led to Bushey Heath High Street, it never bothered me walking alone through a park in those days it felt safe.

The wage was based on commission only and the people were mainly Londoners, wonderful characters. The offices were small, cramped and the blinds were always drawn but I ended up earning a great deal of money for my age, and John and I were able to live off one wage and save the other completely. I seemed to be good at selling on the phone, my dad saw a wage slip one day and said, 'bloody hell you earn the same as me'. I missed Pauline something rotten in those days, but she went on to do much better things, she was always the one who was good at maths and very articulate in her work. I flew by the seat of my pants most of the time, but this company I was working for was very young and growing fast, so fast that pretty soon they decided to move to larger office back in Watford, they were down Vicarage Road where the Watford's football stadium was, again more bus fares and a long walk, but still the excellent wages made it worth it.

My sister Maruja was now married to Roger, her ambulance driver, they got married on the 1st January 1972. The newlyweds started married life living in rented accommodation in Abbots Langley whilst saving for a home of their own. When John and I would visit her at the flat I remember the lovely smell of bread as it was situated next to a bakery. Mum and Dad were very happy, having enjoyed their daughter's wedding, and they were pleased to see me more settled. This relaxed happy-go-lucky life was soon to come to an abrupt end for all of us.

My sister had not been married very long when we discovered Mum's cancer had returned, this time with a vengeance. So Maruja and I took the decision to both work part time. It wasn't ideal as Maruja and Roger were saving to buy a house and John and I were trying to save for our wedding, but at that time nothing else mattered but Mum, she was our priority as she had always been. Dad's job being on shifts was not ideal for Mum, as she would need round the clock care, so it was decided that each morning I would make her some breakfast and then leave for work catching an early bus into Watford, My sister Maruja would arrive to take over the morning shift preparing her lunch then leaving to catch her bus taking her to The Peace Memorial Hospital Watford to start her afternoon shift. I in turn would return home from Watford to be with Mum from 2pm onwards, my sister and I were passing ships but the Rota meant Mum was never alone or wanting for company, I treasured those afternoons and evenings with Mum so much as we did nothing but talk and have fun. She would always chat about her life in Gibraltar as a child, about Spirit world and she talked a lot about her condition. I would cream her body so that she would not get bed sores, feeling her bones through her tissue skin. She was still a very beautiful lady and we loved to laugh a lot, but I would know when to joke and when to keep quiet. Her resting times got longer and longer as her strength seemed to fade. She liked to relive her past as though she were experiencing things all over again and I would simply listen, as I think they were her happiest days back then, back home in Gibraltar, in the sun by the sea that's where her heart was, riding those horses across the beach.

Dad, Roger and John put a single bed downstairs in the lounge one weekend as Mum at times found she could no longer climb the stairs easily, I would draw back the curtains so she could see the comings and goings of the Close opposite, for her, just seeing people walking about pleased her. The television went on for company some days, but it was not her favourite thing to do.

She seemed to be improving a little and it was decided that John and I should have a family engagement party, Mum's idea. It was all arranged; we had booked the hall in Aldenham, near Radlett, as John's parents had lived in that area. Mum made a great effort to come with us to look at the hall and approve details along with John's parents Phyllis and Jack. She was buzzing about it, and with only a couple of weeks to go I bought a beautiful purple dress and I was ready to party. However, the week before Mum's condition rapidly worsened. She was in pain, lots of pain and for most of the time now, she was taking a lot of pain killers, which made her sleep a lot, my heart sank, not knowing if I should just cancel the evening or not, the invitations had already gone out, but family would understand I kept telling her, but Mum insisted it should go ahead, saying Dad would be there, we asked our dearest next-door neighbour's, Hilda and Tom if they would sit with Mum for that whole evening so we could go to the party and I could relax knowing Mum had them with her. Hilda did not hesitate and told me I was not to worry, she and Tom would not leave her alone and stay until we got home, no matter how late it was. What a wonderful friend. I kissed Mum goodbye that evening with a heavy heart and she sent me off with a laugh and a smile.

My favourite photo of my Mum

All the family were there all our uncles and aunties from both sides, Nanny, God bless her tried to pick up a cigar butt with a cocktail stick thinking it was a sausage putting us in fits of laughter and she was complaining the music was too loud, but insisting on sitting in front of a massive speaker, such a celebration night for all the family. Inside my heart was aching to be honest, Mum had let me go out of the door with a smile and told me go on and enjoy myself, as it was also my 21st birthday. Later I visited Hilda to thank her for sitting with Mum and she told me how Mum had broken down in tears when I left. She was so disappointed at not being well enough to go but more disappointed for letting me down would you believe. I did hide my feelings that night as I missed my Mum so very much. The following day Mum was admitted into hospital, I feel she had held out in some way to get the party over and done with. Two days later Dad went down with shingles. As a result of all the stress in him too, I asked Spirit by sending a message from my mind asking please would all the heartache stop, please give us a break.

I would have too many highs and too many lows - it was really difficult to cope with life, Maruja as always held things together best she could, I had hit rock bottom at times, John and his family were very supportive, as was his brother Robert but I felt so vulnerable I gave John a tough time. Visiting Mum in hospital every day and looking after Dad was horrendous, I was so tired and feeling guilty for the thoughts of being locked into some sort of nightmare. Although still part time at work, my afternoons were spent visiting Mum then coming home and looking after Dad, making sure he had an evening meal, and at that time with shingles it was impossible for him to visit Mum in hospital, so she was fretting for him and he her.

When Dad eventually went back to work his shifts were 7am to 3pm or 3pm till 11pm on these late shifts I would come home to an empty house. My faith was being tested every day. Still in hospital Mum's medication was now very, very strong, her body no longer coping, her weight had plummeted yet again, down to less than five stone. Her cancer had spread into her spine and bones, she hurt everywhere, bless her. She was put on a new drug, which, along with her treatment, contributed to research in finding a miracle cure. She was a human guinea pig, I suppose, but if it worked Mum told me it might save a lot of lives. The side effects were horrid - she had a blistered tongue and was in constant pain. I went in one day to find her in a positive mood as she had been wheeled into a doctor's conference hall to talk about her pain management and her condition in general, she said there were many doctors and students there and she was the centre of attention, how brave was that I thought, she had insisted on putting on her lippy on first though.

Maruja would pop onto the ward where Mum was in her break times and lunch times, she knew exactly how ill Mum was, more so than me, it was a lot for her to cope with mentally. When I went each afternoon to the hospital, I suppose I was in denial, I would pull the curtain round and Mum would ask me to do hands on healing. I was convinced in my head Mum would get better, a sort of miracle, like we had when Dad and his brain haemorrhage. God how I prayed - where are Spirit when you need them, I thought.

Then the bombshell hit: My sister took me to one side and very gently told me Mum had just two weeks to live, Dad asked if she could come home as Mum had always said she did not want to die in hospital, no wonderful hospice care in those days either and as Dad had already moved her bed into the lounge, we were ready for her, she had asked Dad move her bed by the window she wanted to be able to see the sky. It was a sunny June morning when she arrived home by ambulance, ironically it was such a hot day we had to draw the curtains as it was too bright for her eyes. Her tiny frame got lost in that single bed she was by now in extreme pain and the many painkillers made her a little agitated. It was killing us not being able to help her more, in fact they said two weeks, but within two days my darling mother had passed away in Dad's arms. I had lost a good friend, a Mum, a laughing companion, a confidante, the mother whom I adored was now gone. Just before she passed, she asked my sister to telephone Peggy Parish, a spiritual medium who Harry Edwards had put her in touch with. Mum must have wanted some words of comfort. Peggy told my sister to ask Mum to imagine herself as a flower opening to Spirit, it took me a long time to understand what that meant. To be honest Mum was getting to the point it was all getting too much, and as the pain worsened, we were very anxious so we called our local GP, but he refused to come out that night. Instead, my sister, being in the know, arranged for a doctor to come straight from hospital to give Mum some morphine which was desperately needed. I shall not name our family doctor at the time, but I will never forgive him.

This beautiful lady my mum woke in the early hours, and passed to Spirit about 5am. The moments seemed to go in slow motion, it was surreal, I was full of anger and upset, emotionally exhausted I expect. I heard a strange noise coming from down stairs, I don't think my sister or I had slept at all anyway. Walking down the stairs looking towards the lounge I sat at the foot of our stairs and saw Roger and Dad cradling Mum in a rocking motion her cries of her pain - will haunt me forever. Then she had gone, it all went quiet, Dad ran out of the house and disappeared down the garden to his shed from where we heard uncontrollable sobbing. Maruja was being comforted by Roger and I sat on the lawn in the middle of the back garden in the hot sunshine and was in a complete daze, our dear neighbour Ernie called over to me with concern, are you alright love, but I could not answer, I heard the front doorbell ring and went round the side to see who it was, expecting it to be John, as I had rung him, but there at the door was her doctor, 'How's the patient then', he said with a smile. I can remember simply saying 'Dead'. I hated him at that moment for not coming when he was asked to, if it wasn't for my sister contacting the hospital and asking a doctor to come out urgently, my mother would have been in agony all night. I will not paint this situation as anything but horrendous - no family should have gone through what we went through. Her frail little body was taken away later that day and we all were just numb. Dad said very little and although John as always did his best to comfort me, it was mission impossible. Roger and Maruja left for home, both exhausted. My John went home after a long day with us as we were all shell shocked and emotionally battered.

The silence in the house was deafening, if that makes any sense at all, Dad and I sat watching television next to the empty bed in the lounge where she had passed away. I had been given some tablets to help me sleep but did not take them, instead I tried to make sense of it all in my head. My dad was watching the television smoking one cigarette after another. Neither of us were talking, we were just in shock I suppose.

My John returned the next day to take my dad to the Chapel of rest; I did not want to go, but when they returned, they both said she looked like a tiny porcelain doll and at peace, perhaps on reflection I should have gone, as it made my dad feel much better, my memory to hold onto was of that terrible pain she was in. Just pain.

They were very dark days for me, I think I lost my faith, to see how she had suffered and for me to ask for help in my head and not receive any answers, that was me done. How could Spirit of let her suffer so much, I even got to the stage before her passing, that I asked Spirit to take her, rather than to see her suffer anymore, then felt guilty for having had those thoughts for a long time afterwards, guilty for being glad it was all over, I had been full of anxiety all the time, maybe feeling guilty for being free when it was over.

My darling Nanny was coming to terms with losing a special daughter and I, at that time, was not able to comfort her in the way I should have, as I was trying to sort out my own grief, we all seemed to be in our own little worlds. Dad was set on working all the hours he could, there was me alone in the house for much of the time, a home that had once rung with laughter and fun, full of love, was now just full of painful memories for me. I can remember thinking that I had to get back to full time work and how I must start to get my life in order, for John's sake as well as my own. I rang my boss, another John and asked if I could go back to work full time, he was very kind and just said, 'See you Monday'. My Johns' family were all very understanding and supportive, but you have to deal with grief in your own way and I was not easy to rub along with. As well as heart ache there was anger in me.

My Mum was loving, very overprotective at times, a lady who loved her family to bits, my time spent with her, especially when we were coping with her illness together was so valued and will never be forgotten. Her daughters were everything to her and Bill, my dad, was the only man she ever loved, she adored him. It was a short life and some would say a sad life. I would agree to a point, it was a life cut short, but I know she left behind special memories and respectful love. She always said to me, "Love, and you will be loved." She and I would laugh a lot, cry a lot and above all share feelings, good or bad. Many times I would sing the Al Johnson song, Mammy, I would walk a million miles for one of your smiles, just to make her laugh. She always had great compassion for others, and a gentle heart.

My Uncles Frank and Sid (mum's brothers) helped to arrange her funeral, it was to take place on the 27th June, (my John's birthday) at the local Catholic church, ironically the same church I had sat in as a child with my Aunty Winnie years before. I could not tell you who attended the funeral, I know it was close family and a few friends, but the whole day was a blur, mum was buried in Garston, Hertfordshire in a double plot so she could be laid to rest with my dad when the time came for him. My beloved friend Pauline was with me that day, helping to make people tea back at the house afterwards, Dad did not want a wake, so after the funeral I popped on a bright red dress as Mum hated me in black.

For a while I lived in a kind of void after Mum's death for quite some time in fact, and my faith was once again being seriously challenged, I wrapped myself up in my forthcoming wedding plans to John. It was so difficult without Mum, but I remember her words to me always and to this day "Love and you will be loved" and that is what I have tried to live by, that simple but meaningful advice. Also trying to hold on to the thought that she was and is now in a better place, pain free, but back then, my home became just a house to live in. I could not understand why God had chosen to take her, my Mum, my friend and in such a manner. My thoughts of her were of her illness only and the last days, and the pain. Somehow, they just would not leave my mind. But life as they say goes on.

Very soon after Mum's funeral I took the decision to get yet another job locally in Bushey High Street at a company called Craig Miller, an office job where I had restaurants to look after in the Chelmsford and Norfolk areas, all by phone, taking their food orders and arranging deliveries. I just needed to change my routine totally, and the women I worked with were so kind and wonderful to me knowing what I had lost, and a family atmosphere was created around me.

It was easier to keep an eye on Nanny as I would pop to her house at lunchtimes or after work, then I would walk home, to cook a meal for dad. My sister also always made sure Nanny was alright and popped in to see Dad often. For me being on my own in the house was increasingly difficult especially if dad was on a late shift not coming home until eleven thirty at night. I would long to hear his key in the door, he was too tired to eat usually, and settle for a cuppa, then I could relax and go to bed.

Many times, I would visit Nanny's house straight from work, dad was on lates any way and if I wasn't seeing John, it was company for me. She was always very welcoming, making me a sandwich and a cuppa for my tea, I would sometimes ring Dad and ask him to pop and fetch me as I hated walking back at night on my own, he had a Honda motorbike at that time which I would pop onto the back of, wearing just a head scarf, no helmet required then, and I would hold him round the waist so tight, more for a cuddle really.

I guess he and I were both feeling lonely trying to support each other, but there was not a lot of communication between us, he was battling his own loneliness. When we got home the first job was to turn the kettle on and then the gas fire in the lounge of that house always seemed so cold and unwelcoming then. We would both sit together to watch television. Not much was said, Dad would smoke one cigarette after another as usual. He was a shy and a very respectful man, conversation was none existent at times between us but as sleep was also difficult for both of us, we stayed watching the television till the announcer said goodnight and the screen would turn blank. To relive this part of my life in this book has been both difficult and yet therapeutic. My Mum was a loving brave, beautiful woman who laughed a lot, she loved people and will always be remembered by her friends and family as a gentle wonderful person who deserved better in life. She had simple pleasures; one was watching a line full of washing blowing in the wind on a sunny day.

My wedding plans were pushing on. I started trying to talk to Spirit again in my head, asking for help, usually it was Mum in my mind when I did this, so I guess I started to get my faith back a little, I was always aware that someone was listening and even went to see a Medium who lived in Luton, at that time, I kept dreaming of Mum, the dream would be of me going on a journey to see her but I never actually arriving, perhaps the medium would give me some guidance from that dream I thought, or perhaps it was some sort of special message she could intemperate for me, but it was not meant to be. No evidence came through, other than her saying your mother is in Spirit, it left me a little cold to be honest, but one piece of advice she did give me, which I pass on in all my private readings, when people had suffered a loss, and like me they had bad memories of their passing which overwhelmed the good she told me this would help. This Medium told me to place my Mum in a happy box moment, a time when we both had fun and enjoyed a good belly laugh together, a moment in time that was just a happy one. Well, there were indeed many laughs and a lot of fun times I could recall, but the medium insisted it had to be that one special moment, she told me to hold onto it and place it in my Happy Box Memory so I did and to my amazement it did help.

My Happy Box Moment was when I used to come home from school, I often lifted the letterbox and shout cooee I'm home and looked to see Mum walking through from the kitchen to open the front door. On this particular day Mum was waiting for me, she intended to blow in my face, but as I lifted the letterbox, instead she accidentally spat in my eye. As she opened the door, we both fell on the floor in fits of giggles as she was trying to apologise saying how she did not mean to do that. It was so funny, hysterical laughter rang through the hall, we both had to race to the loo as we had laughed so much. It was accidental but hilarious and a "you had to be there moment". It was my happy box moment, but I guess there could have been so many, as it always ended with cuddles, but this was the moment I would choose to hold onto. I wish I could have passed this information onto dad as he was holding on to his own demons after Mum's passing, he could get quite low at times, working all the hours and with no worries on the money front to take his mind off things he started to enjoy a drink at the pub, coming home a little worse for wear at times. He would not take the car, but would end up buying everyone a drink and get happy drunk, but never when he was working. He was never an angry man after a drink and I was never frightened by him, but one evening I decided to bring matters to a head. He had been for a few pints with a neighbour and was so out of it when he came home, I had to help him upstairs where he crashed out without undressing on the bed. I popped him into the recovery position, but worried about him all night.

*Mum and Dad at a Bishops dinner dance
in the late 60s at the Top Rank*

I suppose people thought they were being kind getting him out to the pub, but for me this was the last straw. So, when I got in from work the following day, I gave it to him with both barrels, telling him I needed a dad and to get his act together or I would get married and not come back. This was all said in floods of tears, it was a real shouting match, throwing my toys out of the pram moment, but from that day on, he never did it again. I think he realised he was not the only one feeling the pain of losing her and thank God I got my dad back. I came to the conclusion he just wanted to feel needed. We all do, at some point in our lives. I remember asking Spirit for help that night and feeling my prayers were answered. I was not the easiest person to rub along with either. Poor John would confirm that as my emotions were all over the place and I had many insecurities but I needed my dad more than ever.

Spiritual Knowings

Dad with his new found friend Brandy My spirit guide

After that row the air was cleared between us and we became very close. and strange things seem to happen to Dad, for one he got promoted at work so his life was busier and he was put in charge and given a lot more responsibility, his manager, a Mr. Clark at that time, had recognised how many hours Dad had put in and probably saw the need for him to have a sense of purpose, as his work was everything to him after Mum passed. He would stay on sometimes working longer hours than he should have, or covered people shifts if they were ill. I guess he might have thought he had nothing to come home to at times, especially if I was out and about with John. Dad was awarded a gold pen at work as his quick actions one day saved a man's life after he had fallen from a crane on site, whilst doing some building work. We only found out when we found a gold pen and thank you letter in the sideboard drawer.

One evening whilst dad was on a night shift, some of the men said they had heard strange noises coming from Stanmore common, like a howling sound. It was making them feel freaked out, so dad decided to go and investigate. Walking out of what they called The Main Gate, he started walking slowly towards the sound. It was a pitch-black night, and as there were no lights on Stanmore Common, only some lights in the distance that could be seen and the lights behind him from the Marconi Gate House of course. Suddenly in the distance he saw standing quite still a large wolf like figure it was surrounded by a mist or haze, it looked up and stared at him for a bit, then started bounding towards him full pelt, dad stood his ground and never moved, as it got closer, he saw that it was a massive Alsatian dog. When the dog reached dad, he expected it to pounce, but it stopped and sat down in front of him, quite still.

Dad said he just turned very slowly with his back to the dog and started heading towards the gatehouse, stopping to turn and say to the dog, 'Well are you coming?' They walked through the gates together and up the steps to the security office. Once there the dog hesitated, Dad turned again and said, 'Come in then, if you want a drink'. Once inside the dog was given a drink and some food, which they kept for the local stray cat who was a regular visitor, a bed was made up from donated car blankets by the men and an old cardboard box large enough for the tired bedraggled dog to lay down in was found. The dog had been shivering and Dad had given him a tiny nip of brandy to warm him up as the poor thing was so cold, and shaking, Dad instantly knew they had a new recruit and called him Brandy.

After a few days of the men making many enquiries into the dog's ownership, it was decided if he was not claimed, they would indeed take him on as a guard dog rather than him go to the local dog pound, Brandy had a new home, he was a loving gentle dog by nature, but looked the part and made a great security dog. A new collar was purchased along with a nice new dog basket and bedding and a budget was decided upon for his upkeep. The vet's bill was covered by the men themselves, treats and toys followed as all the men loved him, he was part of the team, the security gatehouse was always manned and when the men did their rounds Brandy would go too.

Dad was very excited to have this dog in his life, it gave him a spring in his step and on his day off one Saturday morning he asked if I would like to pop up to Marconi in Stanmore and see his new found friend, as he drove me up to the gate house he told me to wait by the car, I had heard so much about this dog and was eager to meet him. As I stood outside the Gate House by the car waiting for Dad to bring him out, I had a strange feeling of anticipation and to my amazement, as soon as they approached me, I realised I knew this dog. Same large ears, same large head, yes, this was the dog I had pictured at the end of my piece of rope as a child, the dog I would walk and play with, stopping at lamp posts much to my other friends' amusement. My childhood playmate, I think Spirit had sent my dad, my Totem guide to help him. In fact, I knew they had.

10
Wedding Plans Go Ahead

My dearest friend Jo, who had also lost her mother, Jean, to a sudden passing, had always kept in touch and as Jean had been such a good friend to Mum so Jo was a good friend to me, we were all like family. I hope our mums managed to meet up again in Spirit World, enjoying a chat and a coffee as they always did. It is such a pleasure to talk to Jo freely about my Mum, as in so many cases people avoid the subject of your loved ones who have passed because they don't want to upset you, here as all you want to do is talk about them, even though they have gone from your everyday life, it keeps their memories fresh. Many times, since I have done spiritual readings for people, you could see the relief on their faces just to be allowed to talk about their loved one openly and freely and to share a memory of them made it special. If loved ones that have passed are talked about in everyday conversation, they are never forgotten and still part of your everyday life, and you can draw them closer to you.

I found it difficult planning a wedding without Mum's input, but my sister Maruja was always on hand to help and whenever I met up with Jo she too was also a good sounding board. John and I decided on the wedding date it was to be on the 23rd March 1974, mainly because it was my dad's birthday and we wanted him to feel part of the day as much as possible. The church we would choose was St James Church, in Bushey High Street, what I had not taken into account however it was lent and I was not allowed flowers and the beautiful altar and a Golden cross would have to be covered - oh well, I thought not important in the scheme of things, it was the people coming together that mattered most to me.

John and I went to buy the rings in Watford High Street, three rings, two gold bands for us and one extra gold signet ring for Dad which we had engraved with the date of his birthday and our wedding day. John and I were very excited as we had also found a small cottage in Houghton Regis, Dunstable to purchase for seven thousand pounds, would you believe, it was a lot of money in those days, but with our savings and the mortgage in place, it was all systems go. All we had to do was try and enjoy the rest of our lives.

On my wedding day dad was so nervous I gave him a tot of whisky before we left for the church. He was a shy man and hated being the centre of attention and I would not let him smoke near my wedding dress, so the whisky steadied his nerves. We were picked up by a white Rolls Royce and I was so proud of him that day, I think we both had an inner feeling that Mum was with us.

My wedding day - 23rd March 1974

My sister was beautiful as my maid of honour, she was about two months pregnant at the time, so there was the added excitement of a new baby on the horizon, Nanny kept telling everyone she was 74, waiting for the punchline, 'oh really, you don't look it', speech, but it was true she was actually still a beauty for her age. The day went by quickly, we had a very small reception in the church hall next to the church and left for the honeymoon early as we had to drive to the airport hotel for an early flight to Tenerife the next day. I threw the bouquet straight at Pauline, my best friend, and as she caught it, she smiled at me approvingly. We had that special moment. Pauline would go on to marry Ian, a great guy and they had two lovely daughters. I always had and will have wonderful love for her as a friend and confidant.

Left to Right - John and I signing the register.
With my Dad on the day.
My sister, Maruja and I

John drove us to an airport hotel in his old mini which we called Rudolf and we arrived just in time for a late supper and then straight to bed as we had a very early flight the next morning. My John had a Spurs football match on the television in our room with me by his side in bed, 'What a perfect day', he said. Men!!!! Our honeymoon was great it was in a place called Los Cristianos, Liz Taylor and Richard Burton, had stayed there in the same hotel before us booking the top floor for themselves, it was a very quiet area, and remote, the hotel reps told us not to venture out in the evenings alone as there were large pot holes areas about, but we did go for an early evening walk being adventurous, but we soon realised the real reason, we had taken some large oranges with us and walked up to the top of a steep hill but once at the top we were faced with a large pack of hungry snarling dogs looking very menacing, John turned to say to me don't run, but I was already at the bottom of the hill and still running. John chucked the oranges for the dogs shouting fetch and was soon at my side.

Back from honeymoon, (no I will not give you any further details) we settled down to the normal, whatever normal is. John had got himself a job in Dunstable working for a local Builders Merchants Lockhart and Bennett. Every week we would visit my dad sometimes twice a week at first, we usually took him out to the local pub for a bite to eat and a drink, The Horse and Chains in Bushey was his favourite. The fish man would pop in with a large basket full of prawns and winkles and dad would treat us. We loved that, it was only thirty minutes' drive back to Dunstable, so quite doable.

Dad took on more responsibility for Nanny. He was a brilliant son in law, helping with her garden and odd jobs and also made sure she had enough money to get by. When Nanny became ill and was hospitalised. John and I both looked at each other and said the same thing when we saw her lying there in her hospital bed, she had given up, that look in her eyes told us she was ready to go. We got to hug her and I managed to tell her I loved her before her passing. She was late -seventies bless her. It happened not long after we married and I was unable to attend her funeral which upset me greatly but I suffered a miscarriage and still needed bed rest. I thought of her from my home on that day and had my own quiet moment of prayer and talked to her in my head, as I always do now. I kept thinking at least you're with Mum now and Grand Pop. Nanny always felt guilty for Mum passing first, 'Why didn't they take me?' she would say.

I loved my Nanny so dearly and she is always in my thoughts, all she had gone through, yet she always had time to help other people, and was always positive about everything. She did give me a gold locket once and I have worn it round my neck ever since. Inside I placed a picture of her and a folded four leafed clover, which I had found in her garden when I was about seven. She was a funny and vibrant woman of strong principles and faith, I had always admired her inner strength but most of all, she was a loving Nanny that gave you her time and a hug when you needed one.

I was very sad to leave my job at Craig Millar, leaving my band of women who had become such good friends, but the drive to Bushey everyday had been too expensive. After Nanny had passed I managed to get myself a new job in Dunstable High Street, if needed I could walk into work. I became a receptionist at the Local Council Offices, working as their switchboard operator, looking after peoples bus pass renewals, tree preservation orders and general front desk tourist information. Knowing nothing about the area I bluffed my way through as per, and with the help of another switchboard receptionist called Maureen, I survived. Maureen and I became lifelong friends and still see each other often.

Maruja and Roger had bought a house in Milton Keynes which was then an an up-and-coming city in the making, they started their family giving birth to a son and life for her was very hectic. Dad would love her visits, seeing his first grandson, named James after him. The idea of children for me was not front and foremost in my mind at that time, but I wondered if I would ever be able to fall pregnant again, after the miscarriage.

Left to Right - Me, Nanny Celia and my big sister, Maruja

One year we took my dad on a holiday to Majorca and oh boy! We had a party, he really enjoyed it, especially the barbecue we went on, with roasted chicken and pork placed on a spit, and with the waiters coming round the tables pouring sangria down our throats. Champagne was flowing and we really let our hair down. A few lads from our hotel got really drunk and when we were all ready to leave sitting on the coach the rep did the usual head count, and they found one of the young lads was missing, the coach driver was getting a little irritated saying he would have to leave and was going to go without him starting the engine up, when to my surprise Dad jumped up and said he would go and fetch him, he politely asked the driver to wait, and placed a few notes in his hand as an incentive. A short while later he and this young lad appeared back on the bus, everyone cheered and clapped and we were on our way. The lad was completely off his face and looked dreadful. Dad just sat back and enjoyed the ride back to the hotel, without fuss, keeping an eye on the lad sitting next to him on the coach, the Brits all singing *Show me the way to go home*.

The following day we were sitting round the pool when three of the lads came down, all looking rather worse for wear, we had made friends with them and we were chatting and laughing about the night before. Finally, the young man who Dad had helped appeared and went straight over to Dad and shook his hand thanking him for getting him back on the bus and apologising for his behaviour "I was so very sick wasn't I" the lad said to Dad, serves me right I lost my two false front teeth, which were on a plate', giving us all a toothless grin, I was being so ill "my Mum and Dad will kill me when I get home" he told us. Dad reached into his pocket and brought out a large clean white napkin, 'Don't worry son', he said, 'I rescued them for you and cleaned them up'. That was my dad. My pop.

John and I made the decision to move into a bigger house, upgrading to a semi in Dunstable, it was there we started our family. I was twenty seven by now and it was there we had our two sons, David, my first born in 1979, then in my thirties I had Ian in 1982. My sister also went on to have a beautiful daughter Laura, to complete her family. Dad was such a proud granddad and managed well living alone.

I had a bit of a rough time with my first child and whilst in the side room of the labour ward, waiting for a caesarean theatre to become available it was not only uncomfortable but stressful, I remember being very tearful. John had been told by the midwife to go home and come back in a couple of hours, unbeknown to me or the nurses when they placed me in stirrups for the birth as a caesarean was not an option, being short staffed, I had put my hip joint out, and baby didn't want to come out, but none of the medical staff noticed the hip problem, and I though the pain was all part of the process, one of the nurses said to me, 'Would you like me to call your mum love, I recall saying there are no phones in heaven.

Oh, how I missed her at that time. Four hours later at ten o'clock that evening David was born. As there were no doctors there to do a c-section, I had a rough time. Ian three years later was an easier birth, in fact he had to be caught as he shot out like a pocket rocket.

My father loved all four of his grandchildren and he would usually come and stay with John and I in the summer months as he loved to do the garden for John. Christmas was also a time he would come to me usually for the week, he would be happy to sit alone Christmas Eve guarding the presents round the Christmas tree watching television, while we would take our sons to the local pantomime. Dad would eat all the chocolates decorations off the Christmas tree, leaving the empty foil wrappers in the right shape, still hanging there for everyone's disappointment, when the kids went to grab one, it was empty. Dad would say Santa's helpers have helped themselves again, all in good humour, good job I always kept some hidden for the boys. Johns' parents would also join us on Christmas day.

One year I rang dad to make the arrangement to pick him up but he insisted on staying at home on his own which was very unusual, but I respected his wishes, as he said he had a rotten cold and felt he just wanted to stay by the fire and relax and watch tv, I expect being a busy mum I did not read too much into it, saying we would see him at New Year as this was his favourite time and we usually had an adult party at home which Dad loved. Being a Geordie, he would always like to do the first footing with bread and coal.

I rang him the day after boxing day and he sounded dreadful, just saying he had been ill and had difficulty getting out of the chair, so he didn't bother going to bed. 'I am on my way', I said. I drove straight over to collect Maruja from Milton Keynes and we went straight down the motorway towards Bushey, too fast as I recall. We let ourselves in, John had also arrived by then and we found he looked really ill and we managed to get him to bed. We made arrangements for the children as we were going to stay on and look after him, but later that evening his breathing got much worse. Roger, being an ambulance man, suggested we get him to hospital. Dad didn't want to go but we had a duty of care and called them anyway.

His breathing was painful and he was admitted straight onto a ward, it was as we feared pneumonia. All four of us stayed with him, as he passed over to Spirit on that noisy ward with the curtains round us, my sister and I told him we loved him, holding his hands. I whispered to him gently, go and see Mum now; a tear literally fell from his eye and he was gone. It was not the way he would have wanted to go being such a private independent man. I miss and love him so much but know he is with me always.

Maruja and I wept buckets and felt numb, as anyone does with the loss of a parent, it's like being orphaned. Dad was what I would call a man's man, he could be shy but he was mentally strong. If he had a bad tooth, he would pull it out himself, if he was poorly, he would usually ride through it and tell us later. There were many happy moments to remember with my father.

His funeral arrangements were made however as it was the Christmas holidays, we had to wait until after New Year. I asked Maruja if I could do the eulogy and she agreed. Dad was not a church-goer and it didn't feel right for someone to stand up and talk about a man they never knew. It came easy to me, the words flowed onto the paper and life, as they say, goes on, my sister and I were both busy having to look after our children and I was doing a delivery job for a catalogue company. The funeral was just days away. I had most of the eulogy completed but could not remember my dad's fathers name, not being able to get hold of my sister, I intended to call her that night. I went out doing deliveries rushing round, as I needed to get back for three in the afternoon to collect the lads from school, the last delivery was in Houghton Regis, a young woman came to the door, signed for the parcel and as I turned to walk back down the path, she called me back, 'George', she said, 'the name you are looking for, Spirit have told me its George'

Well knowing Spirit as I do, I was not surprised at this. 'Are you a medium?' I asked,

'No', she said, 'but I do get stuff from time to time'. Thanking her, I returned home and as I walked in the door the home phone was ringing. It was my sister, good I said can you tell me the name of Grandad Stanners. "George," she said. I told her of my experience.

If someone needed help my dad would be there, he was over generous with money at times to anyone that needed it. We loved him so very much and always felt in safe hands when he was about. I hope one day I can meet him again, just to say, thank you for being my dad, my pop, my hero. Like the song says I *would love to dance with my father again*.

David and Ian were to stop asking where Grandad was after a while, daily life gets you through the heartache with both parents now gone you have somehow an empty space in you. A feeling of great loss, a feeling of abandonment, and you realise how much you value people after they are gone, I lost the feeling of being safe under my parents' wings, but at least I have had more fun times with my father as he was in his seventies when he passed, unlike Mum taken to soon. John's parents were still alive and at least my sons had two loving grandparents. Phyllis and Jack decided to move to Dunstable from Watford when they retired and were very much part of our two son's lives.

In life there are many bumpy roads, ups and downs and after many twists and turns along the way. I lost a lot of weight when Dad passed to Spirit and went down to under five stone, I was mentally vulnerable I suppose, and was lost in my own head for a while. I lost my way spiritually once again in my everyday existence was a struggle. John was supportive as always and let me find my own way back, in my own time. My world was upside down for a while. John worked down in Devon for most of the week having got a better job, so I was busy with not that much time to dwell on things. I knew I had to get back on track and find my roadmap again. I had lost my way but thanks to the love of my sons and husband and family I did just that. The 80s for me just flew by, the day before one of my sons birthdays the news told us of a disaster, it was 26th April 1986 a nuclear power station at Chernobyl exploded and caught fire it was yet another scary episode, we were not told at the time the full scale of the incident but there was an exclusion zone around that area and is still in place today it's deemed inhabitable many lives were lost and people were evacuated from the radiation zone, some people were to develop cancers, it is still a very radioactive area today and will remain so for many years to come, all animal life died, and many had to be shot by the authorities... The truth eventually got out, as after the initial explosion and fires there was a plume of radioactivity in the form of a cloud that was spread by the wind over countries such as Ukraine Belarus and to a lesser extent in countries in the rest of Europe. For us here in the UK The effects of this were felt mostly in Wales, Scotland, and some Northern English counties like Cumbria, which all experienced heavy rain as the radioactive cloud passed. When you have small children, it is frightening to listen to the news.

Spiritual Knowings

Maruja Dad and I in the cottage back garden

11
The 90s

In the 90s technology took over as computer scientist Tim Berners-Lee, released the source code for the world's first web browser and the internet as we know it was born. Everyone started to get mobile phones, sometimes it was difficult to keep up with the changes. John and I decided to move to a more countryside setting. In the late 90s we wanted to move forward for a fresh start in the millennium year. We had had some tough years and it would feel like a new start for both of us. A local estate agent I knew from working at the solicitors called Stuart, said I should go and view a two-bed bungalow in one of the villages, even though we had wanted to view four bedroomed houses. I was unsure, but as he insisted, I went to view it anyway in my lunch hour. Stuart convinced me I would love it. When I arrived, I noticed the name on the bungalow, it was called Fourclovers. With that gut feeling I clutched the locket Nanny had given me and rang John to say I had found a home for us to enjoy. We both loved it immediately and having come through a very difficult period in our lives it felt right for us. David, our eldest son was now out working locally and Ian was about to head off for university in Birmingham. I had been working for a firm of solicitors in Dunstable at that time, which I loved, but I found myself being head hunted by a friend's husband who had a financial banking company. For me it was very much a new beginning as I found it was a great place to work and I made so many new wonderful, good friends of all nationalities there. I always said if the world could get on as well as everyone in that office, it would be a better place. The millennium was upon us and the new beginnings were meant to be.

12
Millenium Year 2000

John and I in 2000

I got a call from Jo, one of the three musketeers, she asked if I wanted to go to a Spiritualist service in Slip End, Luton that Tuesday evening, we met up on a regular basis anyway for a drink or a meal so I thought why not combine the two go meal first and then onto the church, perfect.

The meal was good and the chat flowed, we always found so much to natter about. We left the pub in plenty of time, having two cars, I followed her as I was not sure where it was, I was imagining in my head how great it would be to get a message from my parents or Nanny so I was a little excited, also I was going to go out of curiosity, as was Jo. I thought it would be fun, a bit of a jolly if you like. I have believed in Spirit all my life and I thought I knew what I was letting myself in for. I had been so busy bringing up my family and getting through life and its struggles with some personal problems, spiritualism was not high on the agenda. I was not therefore prepared for something that was to change my life forever.

13
Finding Spiritual Knowings

The drive from the pub to the spiritualist meeting place was a short one and pretty soon Jo was turning into a lane at the end of Slip End Village in Luton. She drove very slowly past a beautiful church standing back off the lane to my left, but kept driving past it entering through a large gate into an open playing field area, with a sports field with football pitches and tennis courts on the end. There was good parking there to one side and a large brick pavilion at the entrance. I asked Jo if we were allowed to park there and expected to walk back to the church, 'It's in the Pavilion', she said. We're here.

'Are you sure?' I said. Not what I expected at all. Yet as I followed her and walked through the door of that pavilion it suddenly became one of the most beautiful experiences in my life. Not for what I was seeing, but by the way I was feeling once inside, very difficult to explain really, people were busy chatting and laughing, no pomp, no ceremony, just people. It gave me an inner peace; I suppose I knew in my head straight away that this was the church I had been looking for all those years ago when Winnie and I did our search together. All the pieces of the jigsaw puzzle in my head were beginning to fall into place. Yes, it was an ordinary hall, but it was not about the building at all, it was about the feeling, the sense of love and community, it was about people. It was about Spirit.

At one end of the hall there were three chairs where people were sitting ready to receive healing from the healers standing behind them, in the middle to my right, there was an old trestle table covered with a royal blue tablecloth with gold trimmings. Candles were placed ready to light and a simple cross was placed in the centre of the table, so simple but so effective, a banner was hung behind the table and there were two chairs - one for the host and one for the visiting Medium.

Folk soon started to filter in, helpers were still setting chairs in rows placing hymn book on them, whilst two ladies were busy in the kitchen area, putting on a rather large urn so the tea and biscuits could be enjoyed after the service, it was all working like clockwork, no piano in sight. What a feeling of community, there was no fee on the door, it was just donations only to be collected during the service and that was to help pay for the hiring of the hall each week and keep the doors open.

We sat down and to be honest we got the giggles all the usual stuff like imagining someone was going to say "is anybody there in a spooky voice". I was aware of a few familiar faces in the hall, then the couple that ran the church, David and Sheena, came up and welcomed me personally and thanked me for coming, these wonderful people gave up their time each week on a Tuesday evening to run the church doing all the bookings of the mediums and organising the hymns and the healing sessions. David was a bundle of energy, a human dynamo and his wife Sheena a loving and caring lady and actually very spiritual herself. They both had a smile for everyone, they would immediately put people at ease and make them feel very welcome, also making sure everyone who walked through the door was acknowledged.

When the service began David stood up and gave a friendly welcome to everyone and then went into a general chat about something topical in the news, and it was a heartfelt talk with a spiritual message within the content of what he said, he is a knowledgeable man who roused people's spirits and it usually ending up with everyone in fits of laughter. He was not a medium himself working on a platform but he knew a lot about the Spirit World. He taught me later in life that if you can bring laughter in the service the energy would go up, and it was better for the mediums to work in, which I later found to be so true. Jo and I were full of anticipation that evening for a message, a hymn was sung lead by David belting it out taking the lead, a hymn called *Spirit Divine* as I remember, no music needed.

He then introduced a lady called Edna Baker from Luton; she was our medium for the evening. I had not heard of her before that night, a small rounded lady who had the most amazing twinkle in her eyes. She was not in the best of health. Just standing up out of her chair was a challenge for her. When Edna gave her address, I was hooked, as when she started to talk of her spiritual experiences the words captured everyone's attention. In her address she talked of her first real connection with Spirit, when she was working in a church as a fledgling herself, giving messages out for the first time, she said she stood up and nothing popped into her head at all, a sort of stage fright took hold I suppose, but after asking Spirit in her head to help her she saw a young man in her mind's eye, as he sort of floated towards her, she saw he had no legs and when she started to acknowledge him she knew exactly what to say and do. She asked if anyone had lost a son to Spirit unable to walk, and an older couple lifted their hands to say it was their son, Edna went on to deliver his message and indeed was able to comfort them just in telling them he was ok on the other side and he was able to be near them always. What a wonderful thing to be able to do, I remember thinking.

Edna then started to go to different people in the hall, passing on individual messages from the Spirit world, it just flowed, she had a very relaxed manor, not rushing, but with a gentle sincerity. There was no money in what she was doing, no glamour, or big ego trip, she was just working for Spirit in her own quiet way. The evening went by for me, all too fast, Edna worked from seven thirty that evening until nine pm. Jo and I did not get messages that night, but to me it did not really matter, I had a wonderful evening with a good friend and the spiritual experience was the icing on the cake. I did manage a short chat with Edna at the end of the evening as she always made time for everyone, she was so kind and gentle, I said that I had wanted Mum or Dad to give me a message and she told me, they will come through only if there is a need to, and if I was wanting it too much, I might just block them, so her advice to me was to stop getting over anxious about it, they know you are sending love to them just by being here she told me.

Years later I understood exactly what she meant, Edna and I would become good friends, all through my fledgling experience learning to be a medium, I would often visit her at her home in Luton, just as a friend, we would talk about everything other than Spirit at times and then on many occasions she would advise and help me with this spiritual journey of mine. Her knowledge and her own experiences came through in our conversations about life. I never asked for a private reading, for me it was just good to be in her company. I suppose I missed the calm and knowledge of an older woman in my life, sadly when Edna passed to Spirit herself having suffered with illness and the loss of her partner towards the end of her life a family member asked if I would do a short address at her funeral, just talking about her spiritual side, I considered it an honour. She told me once, just stand up and Spirit will do the rest. They will never let you down and so far, I have found that to be true.

I often thank my friend Jo for suggesting that outing that day, for although she personally did not want to continue attending each week, it changed my life and not in a small way as after that first evening I thought about it all that week and when the following Tuesday came around I made the decision to go on my own. Weeks went by and I found I was drawn to that hall and to those spiritual people. I had made instant new friends very quickly and found in no time at all I was offering to help with the teas and making myself useful. I would go straight from work just to get there early, putting the chairs out, like an eager student. Sheena and David were so very kind to me and genuinely good people, they understood how I was feeling and encouraged me to follow my spiritual instincts taking me under their wings. They helped me and countless others with their kindness.

I got to hear of an open circle group in St Albans, so I joined with great enthusiasm, as learning about Spirit World had become my passion and a new found joy, filling a void in my life, and allowing me to gobble up more and more information on the subject. Sometimes when you feel like you are falling through a hole in the snow, something comes along and makes sense of it all.

I was later to become a member of the Homes Countries Association of Spiritual Healers - it was now about 2008. In fact, anything I could read or study was fascinating to me at that time. I even got insured so I was able to be a healer in the churches and started working as a fledgling Medium on a platform to give messages myself. I wanted to be a medium, giving readings in halls and churches and that soon followed. The timing was right, it was something I felt I had to do. The connection to Spirit was there and getting stronger. I was a late starter, some would say at the age of fifty, but that's how it was for me, each time I asked Spirit to intervene and help, they were there for me.

Starting to find things changing within myself was fascinating, I was actually getting thoughts and ideas pop into my head, I would see things more clearly through my third eye, colour mainly to start with and then images as well as thought patterns and pretty soon I was in a group of like-minded people in a small closed circle of six which suited me better. We would meet up on a Thursday evening. We ate a lot of chocolate biscuits and drank a lot of tea but mostly, we had a lot of fun. Taking it in turn to be the host.

It was very important for my development to do good workshops and get advice from experienced mediums, most of which worked in many various ways. I was able to recognise all aspects of this work, which was vital to my progress. If you simply want to open to Spirit privately and get the best out of your own meditations, learn to do it properly and safely. If you want to become a medium you will work in your own individual way. Our circle group was invited to the home of Norma Fox, a lovely Medium who lived in Milton Keynes, listening to her was fascinating as she had so much knowledge on the subject, and had worked herself in churches for years, she popped out a light picnic table and did a circle with us and as we placed our hands on the table an amazing thing happened, not table tipping, but we could actually feel the beat of a heart come through the table.

If you get hooked on this subject, always do your homework, get information and more importantly talk to someone if things don't feel quite right. The second part of this book will guide you through. Meditating on one's own and not really knowing too much, you could find a lot of weird and wonderful things happening, but I was lucky I did not attract bad Spirit. Some learn the hard way, and as long as you do it with respect and protection you will be fine.

David and Sheena gave me that opportunity to learn and develop, I got the chance to do one to one healing in their church and the help and advice from them was always forthcoming together with lots of encouragement, we became good friends and I got my certificate and insurance as a healer so alongside other mediums and healers my confidence just grew.

At First, I found that to stand up and work as a fledgling, (trainee medium,) isn't easy, it's not like you have a script to read, if I faltered, David and Sheena would be supportive and guide me through, they had my back. The fact that they believed in me and my ability was what I needed and I will always be grateful to them for that, it was so nerve racking at first but the people who attend these services are usually patient and kind. I was never made to feel uncomfortable because they knew I was learning.

People that I have seen over the years for readings usually say to me 'How wonderful for you to have this gift' and I always answer, 'We all have this ability, we really do, all that's needed is a little faith and by applying ourselves we can connect to a higher realm, we can we do this by developing our 6th sense. It's very doable'. Place your hand on your heart and go on doing that whilst reading this book, what do you feel, yes, you feel your heart beating this means you're here for a reason, we all are.

14
My Work for Spirit Finally Begins

My spiritual work became my focus and I seriously started to develop and work well doing readings for friends and family, that's a good idea when you start, but I would suggest if you do decide to join a circle group, never stay in that circle group for too long because if you wish to sharpen up your sixth sense, mix it up a bit and if you are not comfortable within that particular circle group change to another. Sometimes one person in that group can have a bad vibe or give you an uneasy feeling, it happens, so change. A person may just dominate the group and ask all the questions, or want things to be all about them, never hesitate to change circle groups because of that situation.

Starting to look at the world from the inside of your very being, is difficult to describe, but once you achieve it, you do get that inner peace you are searching for. You must be clear about your intentions for it is only then, that you can do this work in my humble opinion, you can achieve your personal inner peace and be in your own space. Many people talk to themselves in their head, well that's how I, as a medium, ask for protection. It's easy to simply talk to spirit that way. If you want to be in your own head space make sure it's a comforting place to be.

Spiritual people are wonderful but not perfect, they may lose their temper or they may make bad decisions and let people down in life, but making sense of it all is what really matters and being comfortable with our inner self is what it's all about, having an inner belief is essential. There is a lot of bad press about card readers and clairvoyance in general and it is the butt of many jokes, the way I proved people wrong is to get it right. If you go to see a medium and they are not making sense and you feel uneasy, challenge them in conversation. If it's nothing but guess work you will sense it yourself, or to be fair they may be tuned in to the wrong Spirit and it's not their fault at all, maybe it's not be your message, so tell them and don't be afraid to challenge or just to go somewhere else or visit a spiritualist church.

I have personally found my roadmap and sense of purpose. I started to have more confidence in what I was saying to people and the feedback was very positive and assuring, my inner healing was a big part of this and, again, with guidance I knew it was what I had to do. There was and still is a great deal to learn and for me, sensitivity was the key, it seemed to come naturally to me. I would never give a message to someone that did not ask for one, or lay my hand on someone that did not want direct healing. Please stick to official guidelines and etiquette. When you have had a Rolla coaster of emotions in your own life I feel you make a better medium and have a better understanding of others.

I was standing next to a lady in a supermarket once she turned to me and said, do you know you have a beautiful aura about you, so I smiled and said thank you, but she continued and there is a gentleman that walks with you, would you like a reading at some time? I tried to keep my cool, as I politely declined her offer, thinking I would never do that to anyone. People have to ask you, not the other way round. I have always worked as a result of someone recommending me or directly asking me for a reading, that is the best way. Never attempt to read for someone after you have had a drink of alcohol. Spirits and spirits don't mix, and you're not 100% in control, and if a person comes to you for a reading that has obviously been drinking, I would advise you to decline. I have been asked to go to people's homes and read for up to twelve people in a private session. If they get the wine out, I ask if they could drink it after the session. You have to be firm and work on your terms. Medium Brett Mills and I once worked in a working man's club, we asked for the bar to be closed, until we had finished working, no one actually complained.

One big learning curve for me was when I started doing physics fairs. People would just walk in and have a ten or a fifteen-minute reading, they would walk around the hall looking at the different mediums sitting at individual tables, some of us had banners behind us, some used tarot cards, crystal balls, crystals, ornamental crosses, angels, buddhas and other had items such as dream catchers. I worked with just a packet of angel cards. It was hard work driving to different venues in those days and then as by the end of the day I could hardly talk, not because giving messages was exhausting on the voice, as when you work in a hall you usually have to almost shout to be heard.

Working in churches was what I really enjoyed and from doing that I started to get phone calls for private reading and offers from other churches wanting to book me, that was truly wonderful, if not scary, my diary became full. I would drive myself to the venues and not get home until ten in the evening on many occasions, my sense of direction was terrible and I would usually end up getting lost as some venues were out in the sticks, the sat nav was great and then bang I would lose the signal. I teamed up for a while with another Medium Brett Mills and we got on very well. I would usually prefer to drive and he would help me with directions and for both of us I feel it was a joy to be working together and a good friendship, also it was confidence building for me driving on motorways with a copilot.

Brett and I worked Clubs, Churches Halls and various venues. I loved doing the addresses and I would write Spiritual poetry and Brett would play some beautiful magical flute music straight from his heart which people absolutely loved. We were a good team and would bring a lot of laughter into the services with friendly banter, however, due to my family commitments at the weekends I decided to spend more time with my growing family having five grandchildren at this point. Our partnership sadly came to an end, but we still keep in touch. He is a lovely man and an excellent medium. There was never any competition between us, we were happy for one another, especially if one of us gave an exceptionally good reading. There is no room for green-eye in what we do, and Brett and I just had fun. You have to be prepared for some people to be unkind towards you, and sadly there are people who would like to poke fun at you at times.

At a village hall once, I stood up ready to work, when Brett and I noticed three individuals at the back of the hall sending us up, talking behind cupped hands in uncontrollable smirks and giggles - they had come in to take the P and we knew it. I stopped immediately and said to them, 'Have you got a joke we can all share in, or is the joke me, you can laugh with me that's fine, but if your laughing at me, please leave now', they got up, the gesture was not a wave goodbye and walked out, everyone clapped, I was inwardly shaking, Brett picked up on my anxiety and just stepped in and took over the whole service for the rest of the evening, I hate confrontation. Whatever happens in life you just have to battle through, I tried to remember that quote from Winston Churchill (if you're going through hell, keep going). Thank you Brett for always being so kind.

Spiritual Knowings

Being known now as a Spiritualist Medium I was working independently in churches, and halls but it all had to depend on when I could fit it in around the family as I was still working full time by day, the time seemed to race away, I had my own cards printed and I found my private appointments were increasing but the balance between work and family life had improved. I accepted a booking by another local medium to go and work in a hall called Nash Mill Hall in Hemel Hempstead on a Sunday evening in July of 2014. I don't like the strange roundabout in Hemel and managed to drive round in circles before I found the right exit, typical me, on arriving I was expecting to find a large audience, I was surprised to find just three people there, the lady who booked me herself a medium and two would-be mediums a man and a woman. I felt a little put out at first I loved working to full halls but decided to just do the address and work as usual rather than see them individually, it was strange addressing three people, but they were very kind and I soon felt at ease, the hall was a very old one with a great deal of history to it, built in the 1950s. (like me) There had been a party in the hall that weekend and there were helium balloons stuck to the ceiling. I was giving messages out as they came to me in my head, at one point I asked for a blue balloon to come down for the lady that booked me and to my amazement one slowly worked its way down and across the hall sideways to settle by her side, and remained about two feet off the ground it just stopped. The lady and a gentleman with her, laughed and said 'Don't we get one?' So, I asked Spirit to oblige and slowly one by one two more balloons descended and landed behind the other two people in the hall again two feet off the ground, having had a long sideways journey. They were all gobsmacked to put it mildly, as no other balloons came down that evening and I have to admit, I was just as surprised myself, but then that's the way Spirit works.

My husband John would very kindly offer to drive me to evening services on Sundays as usually, the grandchildren had been with me all day and I would cook for the family. As a result I was a little tired by the evening and John had the patience to sit through the services, always being very supportive. It was nice, as when I finished working many churches sat us both down with a homemade sandwich and a cuppa which allowed us both to chat to the folk who came. I could then sit back and relax on the way home. As John drove we would chat about the evening and how it went, we used to laugh as we realised he was on the Square and I was usually in the circle.

It is my intention to pass on in my book, what I have experienced, in the hope it gives you a better understanding of what being a medium is like. It has been a wonderful journey for me and I think a little knowledge about a subject is not a bad thing, respecting people's advice but keeping an open mind, is for me, the way forward. Spiritualists never cease to amaze me, as they have all had different unique experiences to share.

Brett Mills Joan Hollick and myself at the Queensway Spiritual Centre in Hemel

It is a journey for you as an individual to enjoy and for you to be able to look into your own consciousness this way you can discover about yourself and others around you, what you see in dreams and in your mind's eye, can really be direct messages from Spirit world, we just don't realise it or notice it in everyday happenings when we all have busy lives. It can be a very special way forward for a lot of us, especially when we have suffered anxiety and we have experienced stress or felt lonely at some point. We can stick a plaster on a cut, but being in control of our own consciences, is our own Spiritual sticking plaster for our mind's wellbeing.

There are of course negative things you have to deal with in the Spirit world, just as we have to deal with them here on the earth plain. However, knowing how to deal and cope with them is a must. Negative energy is around us in many forms and we need to be able to deal with it in a safe way.

We have all joked and taken the rise out of someone at some point in our lives, but to take it one step too far and having no thought as to how that person is affected, or what consequences may come from your actions, must be addressed, sometimes sorry is not enough, start to live your life differently, forgiveness is a key and a way forward.

Nothing in my life has been done with bad intentions, it's just how life goes sometimes. I only know we all have a path to follow whatever is planned for us, and it's simply how it's meant to be, our life's plan and our own roadmap. Of course, looking back there were certain things I should and could have done differently but we can all say that.

Between one and a hundred, if we live that long, who is to say what will happen and what twists and turns we make along the way. It very true some things I have learnt the hard way, but everything in this book is from my own personal experiences covering as many spiritual subjects that I feel you may need to know, as they are all linked to spiritual matters and as you go forward yourself you may find you have a special interest in one subject I have mentioned so go ahead and start to do your own research, which would be very beneficial.

There are beautiful things in Spirit world, but it also has a dark side. Always work in what we call Love and Light, simple information, but in my opinion vital. I am not an expert on anything, that's why this book is totally my take on things, but I will tell you of the different stages I went through to contact Spirit. I know a little about each subject and how it affected me on my journey. Now in my 70th year, I have looked back and thought, now is the right time to write this book. To say what I know to be true and to let you open up in your minds your own thoughts and your own ideas and most definitely your hopes and dreams. My background was important to share, as our own personal history makes us what we are today and lets you know who you are. There was a lot of sadness in my life, but also an abundance of good times. My background taught me how to cope with a lot of pain, loves lost, heartache, loneliness and endurance. Thank you for reading so far. Now let me take you into my world of Spirit as I know it to be, because if just one person is costing you your peace of mind it's too expensive. So be in charge of your own mind.

To spend more time in nature and to be more mindful, is something we can all practice in everyday life, opening yourself to the universe. Breathe in the good and blow out the bad. Feel gratitude for every day. Say thank you to Spirit who is around us all the time.

MY OWN WORCKSHOP

15
History

Spiritualism became a movement in March 1848 after three sisters living in New York revealed that they could communicate with people who had died by a series of knocks on a table, their names were Leah, Margaret and Kate Fox. They would work by holding seances and simply talking to Spirit saying knock once for Yes and twice for No and by doing this their proof of life after death took the world by storm, by asking question and getting actual responses, the idea that people could communicate with their departed loved ones was life changing to some, and the Spiritualist movement began. Groups popped up all over the world linking and joining up with that common belief that life does indeed go on.

One of my favourite people to read about was a lady called Helen Duncan, Helen was a working Spiritualist medium she was also the last person in Britain to be tried and sentenced under the 1735 Witchcraft Act. She was born in Callander Perthshire Scotland on 25th November 1897, the daughter of Archibald, a slater and cabinet-maker and Isabella her mother. Helen's talent was rare and exceptional, she could connect to Spirit and she gave wonderful messages from the Spirit world. Helen would travel around the UK and give many demonstrations, also giving many private readings and attending home séances, whilst she was working it was said that her audiences would actually see ectoplasm come from her breath. Word soon got around about her talents; however, this was wartime and pretty soon the Government of the day who were watching anyone for unusual behaviour, discovered that at one of her church meetings in Portsmouth, her then hometown, she gave a message about a deceased sailor from HMS Barnham and revealed that his ship had been sunk in the Mediterranean and that he had lost his life due to being drowned. Word soon started to spread around the Portsmouth community, about this amazing message from the spirit world. It was indeed true; however, the War Office did not officially release this fact to the public until several months later as they were trying to hush up the fact that there was a loss of 861 British seamen when the German U-boat U331 torpedoed the ship. The then Government did not want the morale of the navy to be lowered in any way. The authorities thought of Helen as a loose cannon and she was formally arrested, to shut her up.

It has been said that the real reason for the raid on the meeting house where she was working and for her subsequent arrest, was due to the forthcoming D-Day Normandy landings on June 6th 1944 and the main fear that the Government had, was that she may yet again reveal a date or a location or indeed any other details about their plans. It was of such great concern that they cooked up this plan to get her out of the way, which was decided by the highest levels in Government at that time.

Helen Duncan

It was to be a sensational episode in wartime Britain, Helen Duncan was eventually brought to trial at the Old Bailey in London and became the last person to be prosecuted under the Witchcraft Act of 1735, which had not been used for more than a century. The trial took seven days, and she was sentenced to nine months in London's Holloway Prison. She was even denied the right to appeal to the House of Lords. The local newspaper had painted her as a witch and a spy.

Helen was eventually released on the 22nd September 1944, after the D Day Landings, and it was said, released only with the intervention of Winston Churchill himself. He too, I have read, was a very spiritual man with his own experiences. The harassment unfortunately still continued right up to her death in November 1956. The police yet again raided many private séances, and Spiritual meetings where she worked, as they would seek to find some sort of evidence of fraud, Again and again the police investigators failed in their objectives as there was no such evidence to be found.

Helen had been stressed and was full of anxiety over this constant harassment and in her future years up until she sadly passed to Spirit herself, she knew she would be remembered by some as the last witch, who died, how sad is that. A bronze bust of Helen Duncan, was presented to the town of Callander, but it gives rise to controversy even to this day, by those that hold strong religious objective views, about its public display. As a consequence, the sculpture is currently on display at the Stirling Smith Art Gallery and Museum. She was, as many of us mediums are, just working for Spirit, helping others and passing on messages from Spirit world. It was said, when in Holloway Prison, her door was never locked, as inmates and guards alike would pop in and out, to get comfort from her words and messages from Spirit.

When people ask me that question, what famous person would you like as a dining companion? Past or present, she is one lady I would have loved talking to over dinner as my guest. What a fascinating lady she must have been, oh and Brad Pitt, Harrison Ford, and Robert Redford of course.

16
Talking Spirit

Whenever you do this sort of work, you will find some folk like to mock you, or challenge you. I have been called a white witch I have been made fun of, but I have always stood by the fact that I could sit with someone for over an hour and give them positive, clear evidence from Spirit world, that's proof enough.

People sat in front of me, and their body language cried out to prove it, crossing their arms and trying to avoid eye contact. Saying a definite No to everything, but as a medium you keep going until finally you mention things that get a reaction. I would find at the end of a very long session in private or in church, even though it was like pulling teeth, the person I was reading for who would have said No No No all the time, would then confess to me afterwards in a private conversation after the service that it made sense. WHY? If you can give any medium a little heads up, if they are being accurate and correct tell them YES, they are right. It helps them work and gives you a better reading. Mediums have to trust in what they are given; they cannot change things to suit you.

If, when working, I get nothing, I say so and even in churches I have stood up and said I am sorry I am getting nothing, if you try and make it up, people will soon realise and Spirit will know. I usually got names, or initials, places and pictures of things that were memories for people. Simply pop into my head moments and I would always pass it on straight away, it would be a delight when someone would say, "yes Ted was my husband and Brenda was his mum and Ray his brother", links like that were essential. Pure and simple, family links but good evidence this is what people should expect to get, and deserve nothing less.

My book is basic and I hope it is simple to understand. When I first got involved in Spiritualism, I gobbled up as much information as I could, and you will be amazed at what you pick up just from talking to other spiritual people. The whole book is based on my experiences and my take on things only.

My Experiences

Once whilst working in the beautiful Garston spiritualist church one Sunday Morning, I was drawn to a lady the moment I stood up to work. I got a name pop into my mind straight away and I had a pain in the side of my head, "can you take this" I asked this lady sitting to my right, "my head is really painful on this side", she smiled at me and on giving her more details she said, that was her partner, who had passed to Spirit with a brain tumour quite recently, this was good solid evidence and to see the look on her face was magic, I could see him in my mind's eye surrounded by bright coloured birds, "yes", she said, "he kept a large Avery in our back yard and he loved to walk in and have them fly around him".

Working at a Luton service I went to a young girl and I brought through a young lad, about her age, who had passed very recently. He had been a friend to her from school and she got quite tearful, this amazing lad from spirit world asked for love to be given to his mum as he knew she was close to her, are you close to his mother I asked and she answered yes she is sitting next to me. I looked at his mother who was sitting there in shock I suppose, I smiled at the lady and I asked who is the Martin he is talking about, as he is sending him love, tears came into the ladies' eyes, as she said Martin was her husband, and his dad, he's at home, he did not want to come this evening, that's proper evidence. The lad then wanted them to start to use his bedroom and not keep it as a shrine. But above all he wanted them to know that he was alright and with them in their everyday lives.

Thinking of getting yourself connected? Read on

There are many readings like this I could tell of and like most things that need mechanics to work so does connection to Spirit and Mediumship is a format if you like, rules to stick to and a routine of thoughts. Yes, some find it easy to connect and others have to work at it harder, but the results will be the same and the connections will be there. You don't have to work in a church or hall or call yourself a medium, you can have this connection to spirit in a private way, where death is no longer a thing to be frightened of, you will look at life itself differently, you don't just think about dying as a scary thought you think of it as a natural progression, as we age each stage of our lives is a natural process, we are born, live the life we are supposed to and we die, all of us. and at every stage we do become more aware, that being in our earthly bodies is a privilege, but time does tick away. To believe, and have faith in the circle of life is a great comfort, and the realisation that death can be another adventurous journey to go on.

When you're told you only have ten more years to live, you would probably go into panic and be scared. Now in my seventies I think if someone told me 'You have ten more years to live', I would feel it a blessing, and I would try to make sure that those ten years were lived in a happy way making the most of my time. People, especially nowadays with all the stresses of life, need to get into the right mindset. You don't need to sit high on a mountain or sit alone in a church or a garden to meditate, you can find that peace of mind within yourself. You can be anywhere you want to be, just as listening to music can take your mind back to a place and time in a distant memory that may bring you sadness or joy. Spiritualism can give you that peace of mind you seek, and the awareness of an inner knowledge that you can't really get from anywhere else. So, in going forward and learning about the twists and turns in Spirit world you will eventually achieve that inner peace, someone once wrote…

> *No Meditation, No life*
> *Know Meditation, Know life…*

How true that is, you may be an early riser and have the peace of the morning to think about the coming day ahead, or that person that likes to sit in the evening till very late before bedtime, but even if you are in the middle of a massive gatherings of people around you, just remember your head space is your own and you can take yourself off wherever and whenever you want to be, it's your mind, your thoughts, you're in charge. Reflections and thoughts are yours alone, just as talking to Spirit is between you and them.

Past lives

Many people believe that they have been here before and get a lot of déjà vu surrounding certain situations, places or people, and indeed we have, deep into our consciousness many hidden memories. In many faiths they believe that there is no external soul as Spirit gives us a stream of evolving consciousness. Memories and thoughts come in and out of our minds throughout the day, also in dream state, quite bizarre ones at times, also some fears and phobias that can go back to our childhood or perhaps a past life, it's all there stored away for us to tap into. It gives us an affinity with certain places or people, even animals come to the front. When people have had past life regression sessions, this helps many people to understand why they are drawn to certain places or situations. Unlike the cells in our bodies ageing and changing, consciousness remains the same. All paranormal happenings are hard for us to understand, but just because it is difficult to comprehend does not mean it's not happening.

There are many types of Spiritual Mediumship, all over the world people connecting and practising in their own religions and their own meditations. Do you want to work for Spirit? Or simply meditate for yourself enabling yourself to connect to your own 6th sense, remember this is not a special gift it's doable for all. I can't stress that enough.

I strongly advise that you read about putting your protection in place first and foremost. The second section of this book, the workshop covers your protection, it must be read and put into practice before you start to do anything whether it be in a Spiritual church or in circle groups or on your own at home. When doing regular connection to Spirit it will be an automatic thing to do, so that you are always in love and light and fully protected. Where there is good Spirit, there can be a dark side, this simple protection will keep you safe. It's very rare for anyone to attract bad Spirit if they are simply meditating for themselves or wanting to connect, however a simple ask or prayer put in place first, does the job for protection against any bad energies and our loved ones and our guides and helpers will also protect us, the Gatekeeper who you will learn about reading on, is there for that very reason.

When booking to see a medium for yourself you have every right to ask them how they work, and if they don't have a clue, perhaps you are not with the right person. I shall take you through steps of Spiritual awareness, if a subject means more to you, then do more research for yourself and follow it through. The internet can be a blessing, but make sure you source your information in the right way, there are many Wonderful Spiritual groups within churches all over the county and I don't know one of them that would not be willing to help with questions that you might have on this subject, they have helped me over the years. Your sixth sense will kick in automatically and if you go to see someone and have a very bad reading from them as they are giving no concrete information then I would guess that person could be cold reading you and guessing, don't be frightened to challenge them and say no that's not me, that's not my life, you are getting it so wrong.

Your personal protection prayer

If you are thinking it is a ritual or something complicated you cannot be more wrong, It's simply a prayer or ask no more no less. Wherever you are, just asking for protection in your head and letting your consciousness connect to that of Spirit world is enough, for they are always listening. To start the prayer of protection visualisation is everything, for example if you are sitting at home, just imagine a bright golden band going out of your front door and follow it right round your property, seeing it journey round in your mind and follow it till it has surrounded your house in a circle of light and love, see it arrive back through your front door, bring it indoors and see it around yourself, then you can ask for your family and friends to be included in this protection and mother earth herself. You are protected in that simple prayer job done:

My Prayer

Lord father God
Mother earth
Angels in the universe
Please keep me, my home and loved ones in love and light
Within this band of protection
I ask my loved ones passed and the angels and my Spirit guides
to protect me always
Thank you. Amen.

Anything you might like to add it's up to you. Keep it simple and mean it deeply.

We always use the personification of Mother earth, as she is a living energy.

17
Types of Mediumships

There are many types of mediumships but the three main types in my opinion are: Clairvoyance, Clairaudience and Clairsentience. 'All Clair' means Clear, so Clear Seeing, Clear Hearing and Clear Sensing. I say there are three main types, but each person is an individual and there are many ways to communicate with the spirit world.

We are learning things every day about this subject and there are more and more television programs on strange happenings and spiritual sightings, as ghost hunters have become professional paranormal investigators, some using high technology to seek out more proof and information. Spirit boxes, digital recorders are used as well as cameras with night vision. Specialist SLS cameras that can pick up stick-like shapes and figures that may be in a room but cannot be seen with the naked eye. Also RemPods can be used. They are a device that works by radiating a magnetic field into the environment. If a human or something of spirit origin breaks that field, an alarm is raised. Investigators can also use spiritual voice boxes and by asking questions they can get an immediate response, it is a type of radio at the end of the day, by using the right frequency and signals to get answers, question that an investigator might ask can also be picked up as EVPs (Electronic Voice Phenomena) these can be amazing. Years ago, just called white noise.

All fascinating stuff, and the high-tech equipment used together with good mediums and investigators make excellent viewing. I personally like the ones where they not only find Spirit in the building but they go on to help Spirit that wish to go through to love and light, as in some cases, someone who had passed over may still be residual energy and trapped here for some reason, going over what they did on the earth before they died. We have come a long way from the simple taps and knocks on tables for communication.

An experienced medium can usually get a feeling of a place or building just by their connection with their yellow chakra (gut feelings) and Spirit guides that kick in, from the other side, you get an idea how haunted a building may be and what spirits still remain, and to get answers, through the modern voice boxes is incredible as usually they give direct replies to questions asked, amazing stuff. Simple questions like what's your name and why are you still here, how many spirits are here and more importantly why have you not passed through to the light or what is the problem, simple but very effective. There may not be a problem, spirit may just want to communicate with us or remain in a building they were familiar with.

Stop thinking of mediumship as a gift or a talent, it's within us all, use the gut feeling and go on information given to us by Spirit directly. The Native American Indians had a tradition which would be in the form of a ceremony to ward off evil spirits from their lands. More recently spiritualism has gained even more interest via the wellbeing movement where people will cleanse living space or working space from all negative energy, and help people to find an inner peace within themselves. On a number of occasions, I have been asked to visit properties at people's requests. I go to a house they intend to purchase just to check if the vibe is right, and I have also visited houses where people are a little uncertain if they have a spiritual presence in the house.

My Experiences

Whilst in my first circle group years ago all six of us went to a lady's house in Luton, bless her she saw faces everywhere in her home, in the walls, the tiles, the glass and the wood. She thought she was going crazy. She mentioned the house had been built on an old factory site, and as Spirit hate renovations or disturbance of any sort, perhaps they were unhappy, we did a circle and showed the spirits the way forward into the love and light then smudged the property to release the bad energy, she did not seem to have any trouble after that. She took a lot of comfort from the fact we too, could see the faces, and we all seemed to feel no negative bad energy.

John and I went on a Masonic weekend in Stratford-upon-Avon and we stayed in a very old hotel, which was built in the 1500s and parts of the hotel were being renovated at that time. Again, a thing Spirit does not like, change or disruption, our room was in the old part of the building and on the top floor, the floorboards creaked as you walked on them and the wood was very dark and aged. I had felt the energy in that Hotel the moment we arrived, but thought no more of it, as the schedule for that weekend was a busy one, that night I was lying in bed and saw a rather beautiful serving girl in a maids outfit approached my side of the bed she was dressed in black and white, with a low cut neckline and, she seemed to be carrying something on a tray she wore bright red lipstick and had rosy cheeks, she was really quite beautiful, her hair was very long, hanging over her shoulders. Then out of nowhere I got the feeling of a thousand rats running over the bed. My heart was racing as I felt the sensation of all these nasty rats running, I even felt the weight of their scurrying bodies, it took me a long time to get back off to sleep that night. I told John in the morning and he suggested I research the hotel, so when we got home I googled it and found out that a quarter of the population in Stratford upon Avon died of plague in 1564, William Shakespeare was an infant child at the time and escaped the area. The feeling of all those rats running over me was horrible. It was so real, but at least I understood what I had experienced, but I would not like that to happen again.

Clairvoyance – Clear seeing

This is being able to see Spirit as a person here on the earth or see Spirit in your mind's eye, (the Third Eye). Clairvoyance helps you actually see things that are not perceptible to others, past, present or future may appear to the clairvoyant person, it's a lot of visionary work.

I have to stress that everyone works differently and Clairvoyant people will have their own take on this, and how they individually work, no two Mediums work in exactly the same way. I can get pictures in my mind's eye, and I see faces and then places, or situations, but at that Hotel in Stratford that night I actually experienced a full-bodied apparition. Clairvoyant people may see people and events that are distant in time in the future or past happenings. They have the ability to have a remote viewing, like a video playing out in their thoughts and dreams, much as a physic person can. Predicting a death or a disaster, or impending illness can be stressful, but a lot of Mediums carry this burden, and it would be very rare for one to give out any information of impending doom, even in a private reading, due to codes of conduct, some say they have second sight and are visionaries and prophets. Nostradamus was famous for his prophecies for the future. Nostradamus was not only a diviner but a professional healer to and his life and writings continue to be a subject of media interest to this day. The scientific community widely considers parapsychology, and include now the study of clairvoyance,

My Experience

Sensitivity and understanding should be top of the list in this type of work, Mediums are not there to judge people or situations, they should have a duty of care to help in a manner that's not judgmental if they can, and they are not fortune tellers either. If you sense someone is going to have a rough time of it, you can say it, but in a way that won't alarm the sitter, such as you are going to have a bumpy ride ahead, but your Spirit guides and helpers will see you through these situations and tell you what to say, as usually whatever is ahead of us is in our life's pattern anyway. Spirit will see you through the tough times I know. I have seen so many weird and wonderful things in meditations and also when just going about daily life, one evening I had a gentleman in black just walk through my conservatory. It was not alarming to me, as I could see he was busy going about his everyday existence. He did not turn to notice me, just kept walking through the wall and towards the garden. Many times, in the middle of private readings, I see and sense galloping horses, dogs, cats, and people who would pass through it became just normal to me. Having a drink in our local pub one evening, I told John there was a Spirit cat in the restaurant, he just laughed, and just as he was about to answer me the lady on the next table jumped up and said 'I thought a cat had landed on my lap', John thought this was hilarious.

Also, one night I woke up to find a tiny gentleman sitting in an armchair by my bedside. I do not have an armchair in my bedroom, I did not know who he was, he was not doing any harm, so I turned over and said goodnight, that's how relaxed you can become about seeing such things and knowing you are protected.

Clairaudience - Clear Hearing

This particular psychic ability is when the medium can hear voices in their heads and in their ear directly, clairaudient messages enter the inner ear or come from inside their head. These messages are usually in the form of a voice or it may also be a certain sound, a ringing noise or music even in their ears. Psychic mediums are also able to identify and distinguish these different messages, from their own inner voices in their head (their thoughts), versus the messages they are receiving from Spirits or their Higher Self. Clairaudience can be an external experience too, although this is not as common. When this happens, it may be because a

Spirit is sending out an urgent message, such as stop or slow down or simply watch out!" or they may just call your name, in this way the Clairaudient medium or person can communicate with Spirits that might have lived years and years ago and also be able to contact different dimensions, sending out their thought patterns and asking for a response.

One of the most loved and well-known Clairaudience Mediums was Doris Stokes and she worked in this way, hearing voices in her ear. I have read many of her excellent books, where she was assisted by the wonderful Linda Dearsley. Doris would actually have conversations with Spirit and they would give her answers as a direct communication simply by the voice in her ear, I have always thought it wonderful to have a direct phone line to Spirit world, she would sometimes play to large theatres, what a wonderful lady, her books are definitely worth a read.

My Experiences

I have had the experiences of this myself, but did not wish to work for Spirit in that way and told Spirit so. You must be master of your own mind, and your own consciousness, being fully in control of yourself, and just by telling Spirit how you wish to communicate you can move forward. First time it happened to me I was sitting in my lounge; it was very warm day and sitting with my back against the window feeling the warmth of the sun on my back through the glass I heard quite clearly, 'She's got a large bum', followed my giggles well my goodness that was not very nice I thought looking around to see who had said it. Then I realised I was completely alone. Where I live is very quiet and there was no doubt in my mind as to what I had actually heard, I realised it was spirit voices, I was shocked as I heard further giggles and muffled words, I said in my head straight away, 'Do not contact me in this manner again thank you', and it ceased, occasionally I have heard my name being called, and the odd thing called out, but it is not a regular thing.

Waiting for John to get home from a Masons meeting one evening, it was only about ten o'clock, and I had an early night, he had not been well that week so I knew I would not get to sleep until he was home, I was propped up in bed waiting to see the car lights on the drive when suddenly I heard music like someone had popped a radio earpiece into my ear, it was really quite loud but again I was not afraid, as I then felt a white light over my head that beamed straight on me and a most overwhelming feeling of pure love just hit me, not sure how long it lasted, must have been a matter of moments, it was so beautiful. The music I heard was unusual and not like anything I had heard before. It was soft music. I slept very well that night.

Clairsentience – Clear Sensing

Well, I am on totally firm ground here as this is the way I work, when you sense Spirit, and feel Spirit, it's a knowing, it's probably the way of working with the most types of connections, everyone is Clairsensing all the time so I must point this out it is not unique to me. How many times have you walked into a room and thought I don't like it here, or the first time of meeting someone you just don't like, for some reason. Or in the reverse, you connect well with a new person in your life as though they are your soul mate and yet with other friends, they are just not on your wavelength straight away - it's all about vibes. It is all about sensing, feeling and the knowing.

A lot of this is done by seeing through the third eye and all the senses combining into getting patterns, faces, feelings, and some feelings such as great pleasure or some pain, you become aware of tastes and smells. This extrasensory perception or ESP, also called the sixth sense, is the ability to receive information, which cannot be gained through a physical sense. You have probably** had it without realising. Think of a friend long enough and they will call you, try it. I would sense pictures in my third eye and then I received messages with pictures and patterns coming directly into my head, not direct conversations with Spirit world. The pictures I received were like on a video or thoughts popping into my head as ideas or deep thoughts you suddenly remember, but in a very subtle way, as Spirit nudges you, then guides you and then I am given a thought sometimes by association. In one reading I could smell fish and chips and found out that the person's dad ran a fish and chip shop after the war.

I would get an ache in my leg, and find out where the person in spirit had a leg injury. It's a very gentle nudge but all the time it was giving me the information about the person who was trying to get through to communicate an important message. Initials would also show themselves to me or numbers, but above all names popped into my head thick and fast when I started working too many sometimes. Even names in another language would be presented to me in some fashion, and I loved to get personal nicknames.

My Experiences

I use to go and watch a lot of Mediums work in churches all the time when I first got interested in Spiritualism, one evening a Medium stood up and said I am terribly sorry I have an itchy nose and her nose was really twitching, we all laughed and she carried on, and said still rubbing her nose, can anyone take the name Issy? A lady lifted her hand up and said that is actually the name of her rabbit which died that day, oh my gosh, we all fell about in fits of giggles, not about Issy passing to spirit but the realisation that even animals get their messages through. I have found that when dogs are in Spirit and come to say hello to their owners whilst having a reading, I get extremely cold legs when they arrive.

For one special lady I read about how I could clearly see many green balloons flying into the sky, which unbeknown to me the family had released lots of green balloons as a Remembrance Day gesture. I also read for a beautiful lady who was in her eighties and I kept seeing tartans, so I said 'I am sorry, but who liked tartans? Have you got Scottish links?' she smiled immediately and said no Scottish links at all, it was her young granddaughter who had passed to spirit far too early, through me she was contacting her grandmother to recalled the fact that she loved The Bay City Rollers, and as a treat her grandmother had bought her lots of posters and bibs and bobs, all in tartan. Then I said 'She is with Tom, do you know who this is? her eyes flowed with tears as she said, 'That's my husband who's just passed'. A special day for me as she was clearly comforted to this lady that they were together now in Spirit World.

Psychic Mediumship

I have often admired Psychic Mediums in their work as they can use their extra sensory perception on things and look into the future or the past using a sort of telepathy, some making predictions, and having visions through the third eye, it's a very strong telepathic way of connecting. This ESP, is not only predicting people's future but they may have the ability to look into the unknown, in my humble opinion to be psychic mediums there is a cross to bear. Looking into past situations they have been known to help the police with their ongoing missing person files.

My Experiences

In my first circle group, I had this experience getting a vision of the face of a beautiful young girl child on the front cover of a newspaper and the word 'Murder', in the headline letters along with a picture of her in my head she had fair hair and was almost angelic to look at. I shared this with my circle group in our after-circle chat the following week on the front of a national newspaper where I saw the very face that I had seen in my mind's eye in that Circle group the week before. It was a front-page story, with the headline Murdered. I asked Spirit not to do that again, it was deeply upsetting for me, I cried buckets and it actually disturbed me for weeks. If I had known the victim's name, would it have been preventable? People I know that predict things, must get very strong visions and to see a disaster unfolding in your head, before it happens, for me would be a constant nightmare, such as accidents or murders. With me it's usually volcanoes or earthquakes. I would dream of one and then hear of an eruption somewhere the next day.

A gentleman who lived in the Aylesbury area came for a home reading. It went well and to finish we just sat chatting for a while, and I said afterwards, we have a very angry planet at the moment and that there will be extreme weather and earthquakes. The next day Aylesbury had an earthquake which was felt in Eaton Bray and the surrounding areas. John and I ran outside when it happened as we thought part of an aircraft had fallen off and put a hole in our roof. It was a real loud bang. The man rang me in the afternoon and said, "Well young lady you said we would have earthquakes but I did not expect it to happen quite so soon or indeed in Aylesbury", and we both laughed. Predicting a friend's twin girls is one thing, as it's such a happy event, but predicting disasters I am not sure I could cope with that all the time.

Trance Mediumship

I feel very strongly that one needs to know what they are doing when attempting Trance mediumship and should be quite experienced before they attempt this, as you are actually giving Spirit permission to take over your own body for a while, and allowing them to channel through you, messages from Spiritual world, they may be words of wisdom and teachings, that you are receiving, however it is very important that another person is present, preferably a medium, someone who exactly knows how Trance Mediumship works just in case you run into trouble, such as going in too deep, for if this should happen they can step in to help you out of trouble as it could become a difficult situation, but this I must say is very rare. When you do this type of work you would always first ask your guides and helpers for protection first so then and only then can you begin your communications. These experiences with Trance Mediumship can also allow the sitter to talk in tongues, or they may come out with beautiful poetry. Quite often they would be heard talking in different accents or other languages, fascinating to listen to. Their voices may change, sometimes becoming very deep in tone, but for me what's fascinating is the extent of the knowledge and teachings that are brought forward from Spirit world. I would recommend a trip to see a demonstration. Talking in tongues is just to us an unknown language, and the blending of two energies, if the connection is very strong the person may appear to be asleep, but they are in a trance like state, however, to do it properly they should be in control and well protected. Spirit just uses the medium or person doing Trance Mediumship as a vessel of communication. The meeting of such minds can be extraordinary.

Transfiguration

This is very similar to Trance, but usually done as part of a team within a circle group, as a demonstration, you just invite Spirit to be around you. The Sitter, should be ready to communicate and can ask Spirit to step forward and show themselves by inviting such a strong energy close to you the transfiguration begins, spirit do not actually take you over in any way, you are wide awake and in full control. The Sitter should be in front of everyone sitting in a chair comfortable and relaxed; allowing the other members of the group to see the changes in the sitters face, such as different forms come over their face and a different face then starts to form. It is best to do this exercise with a soft red side light or gentle light only in the room by the side of The Sitter, so the ectoplasm can form and be seen more easily. The people in the circle group just sit and stare at The Sitter, first they will see their face fade completely as it becomes almost translucent and then the magic begins. On occasions many faces can appear one by one quite rapidly. Features like beards and moustaches can be clearly seen. Objects like glasses or earrings, pipes or hats appear as part of the face builds up. The hair can change shape being shorter or longer and the size of head, even the body shape can alter. You need to see it to believe it, it is not an optical illusion as many people in the circle group will be able to look at the ectoplasm forming on their faces. Things change before your eyes. All Spiritual individuals that appear over the face of The Sitter can be asked questions by the circle group. It is very fascinating to see. And The Sitter will be able to answer any questions put to them by the circle group everyone begins to understand why that particular Spirit had the need to come forward. Some do this by mirror staring and you can get the same effect.

Ectoplasm

Just to explain a little about this as many people are frightened of the word Ectoplasm. It can be seen as a light-coloured substance that is said to exude from the body of a Spiritual being when some Mediums work it may just appear and take the shape of a face, a hand, or a complete body. It is normally visible only in the darkened atmosphere of a séance. Ectoplasm is said to be the substance in the involvement of materialisation of spiritual body energies, it needs energy to form and so has a gradual build-up, and at the end of a séance the ectoplasm will disappear. It can leave a sticky residue when left on an object where a spirit may have been, most commonly hand prints can be seen on mirrors and windows. Pools of water also appear at times when spirits are close.

Psychic Scanning

This is tuning in to the other realms and other dimensions from our own minds as I like to think of it, seeing pictures that Spirit world want us to see from the other side or you may just experience short bursts of visions like a video playing in your mind when it happens, it's very rewarding. Spirit contacts us in many ways, but to show us events in our minds can be stunning. Healers can use this seeing colours when body scanning and if someone has gone missing and disappeared without trace, even police have been known to ask a Medium to do some map scanning to try and locate that missing person, with the aid of a pendulum also. Psychic scanning or remote viewing is used quite a lot in those cases and enables a medium to look beyond what would be normally possible.

Many Mediums who are very good at art can draw a face or place just by letting their hands be guided by that of a spirit guide. Artists have been known to draw rapidly and, in some cases, upside down, and then the paper is turned round to view a full perfect portrait or picture. It is, to my mind, a way of the spirit world being able to tune into our consciousness and allow that energy to flow. For me psychic scanning may take the form of short bursts of visions, like a video, of a place or situation but it's very rewarding when it happens, usually before I sleep.

Visualisation

This is being able to see in one's own mind, pictures and images clearly and in many meditations we have to visualise step by step journeys taking ourselves to a quiet safe place where we can completely relax and connect, you can practise psychic scanning by simply looking at a painting on a wall or a picture from a magazine that you like and visualise actually going into the picture and walking around and seeing in your mind's eye what is there and attempting to see what is round the corner of the picture and beyond.

My Experience

My first encounter of psychic scanning was a scene where I could see myself flying over beautiful buildings and green fields, looking into deep valleys seeing the depths and different dimensions of them. When it happens, you realise how special it is and not having experienced it before it's quite unique. The sensations and sense of colour is very vivid, it felt a bit like flying, I was not weighted at all, just energy. My emotions were heightened and I could have openly cried, and as I felt so elated at the experience.

Beautiful music can come through your mind, taking you totally in the spiritual zone for that moment. It clears the clutter from your mind and you are able to balance your chakras. People usually rant, rave and explode about things because they are stressed or imbalanced in some way. By changing our attitudes, we can control this much better and get rid of the negative feelings and start to maintain a stronger balance from ourselves. Your central core and moral compass will be in harmony.

I have a painting called Embarkation by Denis Lawson. We purchased it years ago whilst on a holiday in Swanage and it reminds me of my mother's evacuation from Gibraltar, it's bright and colourful, and drew me into it straight away. For meditation I can imagine getting into that picture then I go on an adventure, letting my imagination fly. Sitting on the boat watching the land disappear into the distance, so relaxing. You may wish to meet a loved one there that has passed over, or simply see what occurs. Visualisation allows your mind to stretch and fly. Many of these holy men you see sitting in very crowded places are not affected by the noise or crowds; they just simply stay calm by visualising and enjoying their inner journey, totally unaware of the hustle and bustle around them.

When you look into the past way back in 1958 top secret agencies would look into ways of enhancing the human brain power, and mental ability. Remote viewers can look into space and time, and sometimes penetrate buildings to see within, from their arm chairs at home. President Carter of the USA got these types of psychics to help when in 1995 a Russian plane came down in the Congo now known as Zaire Africa and they were successful in pinpointing the spot where it was, also in the 1970s an organisation called Stargate in America had a number of secrete projects all regarding remote viewing, all run by various intelligence services. The human mind can indeed project itself into time and space of that I have no doubt. Psycho Energetics will be looked into I'm sure as a way forward, but I cannot help feeling uneasy about it.

Psychometry

A Medium can connect to spirit using psychometry by holding a personal item, that had once belonged to a loved one who had passed over to spirit, it may be an item of jewellery such as a ring or a watch, many people would bring me photos placed on a table upside down, which I would lay my hands on top of to try and trigger a memory links, all items hold energy and have different vibration. Everything that is touched in everyday life has an aura around it, and will hold onto a stored energy field. I find when going into a building for instance, sometimes if I place my hand on the wall, as I sense the properties energy.

My Experiences

John and I once visited The Palace of Holyrood house in Edinburgh, Scotland, we did the usual walkabout with handheld listening earphones, as the place was steeped in history, it had been a palace since the 16th century, but originally it was a monastery. Walking around I could feel the atmosphere was quite heavy in certain areas, and as part of the tour people had to climb a small tight spiral staircase leading to Mary Queen of Scots private chambers. Whilst climbing these stairs I had, what I can only describe, as a panic attack, I could not wait to get to the top and off the staircase itself. John was laughing as he came up behind me saying he had never seen me move to fast, we live in a bungalow and I don't do stairs these days, but I explained to him how very uncomfortable I felt on the way up and had to get to the top fast and indeed once at the top I felt much better but headed for a welcome visitor's chair which I grabbed, sitting there waiting for my heart rate to improve and calm down. Now composed and heart rate back to normal. I popped on the headphones to hear the next part of the commentary on the history.

The recording stated that on the 9th March in 1556 The Queen, some of her ladies and her private secretary David Rizzio were dining in a tiny supper room, which was in the turret just off of the bedchamber, that John and I were sitting in, the recording in my ears went on to say that the Queen was heavily pregnant at the time. Suddenly her then husband Lord Darnley filled with jealousy burst in and stabbed David Rizzio and when Rizzio tried to flee, he was dragged through the chamber and dragged down the staircase being stabbed a further 57 times. I am convinced it was that terrible residual energy which I had picked up on. John and I looked at each other in amazement.

I found over the years that I was aware of Spirit a lot and as a child I would instinctively know when someone had a problem or if something was wrong. Seeing spirit faces in materials such as wood and tiles, brickwork and stone all the time. I was also aware of shadow people and as I got older my spirituality grew, there was indeed a sharper awareness of everything Spiritual which became increasingly sharper. Spiritualism was never at the forefront of my everyday life growing up, but it was mainly with my Mum as a younger child, that I would ask questions and talk about the subject, especially when she became ill, and we had the time together to talk. She passed onto me a lot of her knowledge. I asked if she would contact me when she passed to Spirit, and Mum always said 'No, I will hopefully rest in peace', and be in love and light and we laughed, and she has never contacted me directly since her passing so I take from that she is at peace. And I know (there is no time in spirit world) as we know it, when she passed over, I was very young, and as I have gotten older I have had to wait to see her again, she on the other hand my mother will not of had to wait to see me, I will simply pass through and meet her again, of that, I'm sure.

As we ourselves get older we question things more, and when I did start to question things seriously, at the age of forty plus to my amazement I started to get answers in my head. Never worry if you don't get messages from loved ones - it's not that they don't love you or care about you, it's that they are in love and light and having happy times there. They have let go, just as we have to move on, none of us wish to die, but it is indeed a journey we all have to make, and I have no fear of that.

As a Clairsensing Medium I know what Spirit is around me, I also sense when my guides and helpers kicked in, as they help to bring forward the Spirit of a person that needed to get a message over to a loved one here on the earth plain, sometimes it was not a great long message, just guidance, maybe a little nudging in the right direction, for that particular person at that time in their life if things were tough and they might have been coming off the rails and they needed to get back on track. I never judged anyone, as I have made quite a few of my own mistakes along my life's pattern.

Not working with a direct voice in my ear it was done through thought patterns, a name or place would pop into my head, sometimes Spirit would give me a memory, a bit like in a scene from *Harry Potter* when a memory was pulled out of someone's head to view. So, for me when the person who was receiving the reading acknowledged what I had given them it was indeed magical moments for me and when you give them information that's spot on - job done. You should only give what you are given and not add your own opinion to it.

It's no good seeing a medium that says "mum's or dad's in Spirit", you have to give names, places, odd memories and it is indeed in the detail, such as a personal memory that will make the difference between a good reading and a bad one, something the person can link to, an unusual thing but it's something private for them to understand.

There is a great deal of protocol and responsibility with what Mediums do, and I was ever mindful of the fact that the person I was reading for had a private life and may not want me as a Medium to blurt out cringe details about their lives in front of people in a hall, or even in a one to one privately you should always tread gently.

I have sat and cringed at times hearing other Mediums on platform say 'Have you had a miscarriage', an omg moment. There is always a better way to ask that question? has someone in the family had a baby pass to Spirit that may have not gone full term. That's the correct approach.

A Medium filled me with horror one evening when he said to the young woman he was reading for, 'I have a man in Spirit, he was very close to you, could this have been a love match?' It was again an "omg" moment, that lady may have her partner sitting next to her, so many things and responsibilities to remember when you are working on a platform. To hear a spiritual Medium, tell a young girl that a man is always with her, is ok but the look of horror on her face as he went on to say, he likes to sit at the end of your bath'. OMG - poor kid she must have gone away thinking all sorts, and it was of course utter rubbish.

Thankfully all the mediums I know personally, would not do this and behave in such an improper manner. We are living in a suing society and I was insured to work in front of an audience and to do healing always. There is a code of conduct that all mediums need to use.

You may well ask the question: does anyone really know what happens after death? Well, many people who have had Near Death Experiences say they walk towards a white light, but there are many different stories, the truth is none of us really know do we until we die. Some Near-Death Experiences are reported to be wonderful meetings with passed relatives, some see beautiful panoramic views with perfect locations. People have sensed a floating feeling; each individual is different and their stories do vary. I am afraid to say, there are those who may not have such a good experience. But it's good to ask questions and to be clear about what you believe in, then the fear goes and you can go through life not worrying about your final journey. Answers become clearer in your head and your take on the afterlife becomes more defined, so you can be more relaxed about it. I found people would ask me these questions a lot in workshops, so it's better to have a strong opinion on the subject but always be prepared to listen as others may help with your conclusions. Manifestations of Spirit in an earthly body are very rare, as once you have passed over, you are, as all spirits are, pure energy the contact is purely from their consciousness to yours, when they do get to be seen they are called ghosts, I feel it is the residual energy crossing into our dimension. Spirit needs a lot of energy to achieve this.

My Experiences

One night I was just beginning to sleep you know that drop off feeling when I felt myself float up to the ceiling, it was the strangest thing, I had no fear I have to add, but I was astral travelling as they call it, being awake and aware of what was happening I actually said in my head wow where are you taking me, strangest thing I could see myself lying in bed with John beside me and yet here I was floating about like a helium balloon, but my mind was strong and I said please put me back, and very gently I returned to the position in bed, yes it was strange, yes it was weird, yes it was absolutely wonderful, and No, I did not dream it.

Reading for a young person about five years ago they told me they did not want to be refer to as he or she, and they were somewhat surprised at my reaction as perhaps they were expecting me to react differently I suppose, Things were not going well for them at that time and many challenges lay ahead, I could tell they were a little lost and had angry in themselves for some reason, finding it difficult to fit in everyday life and in general things were tough for them and a daily challenge for them.

I don't know what they expected me to say, but it was clear to me, clear as crystal, I had it confirmed in my mind, so passed it on, we are all unique, we all pass to spirit world, when we pass through to Spirit, we are pure energy and neither he nor she, just energy. If someone does not identify with any gender that's how it is, Angels are neither he nor she just energy, we laughed and they said they were happy to take that on board. Be happy with who you are, and have that inner peace.

Here's some questions to ask yourself - the answers are my own personal opinions, what are your answers?

Does it really matter if we are cremated or buried?

I think whatever happens to our body after death does not really matter in my own personal opinion and personal preference as to your being cremated or buried. I feel deeply that when we pass over into the Spirit realm, all souls are first released at the point of death. The body stays behind, and the brain stays behind, however our spirit, our soul, our consciousness, our very being if you like, is disconnected with all earthly ties and you become pure energy, entering the world of Spirit.

Some see this transitional energy leave the body like an ectoplasm or orbs and rods of energy, unexplained lights, or shadows. Personally, you can stick me in a wheelie bin, in a black sack. I would not need that earthly body anymore, so why would I worry, I would be a free spirit. I liken it to a caterpillar turning into a butterfly - a metamorphosis. You become pure energy entering the light.

Yoda my cat stretching out at the foot of my bed

Suicide?

People who decide to take their own life for whatever reason are not judged in Spirit world. They may have decided to jump off the roundabout of life early, but they were clearly not in a good place here and wanted to escape life as they know it, or in many cases it's a cry for help when they don't succeed, we all have free will, yet if we terminate our life's contract early, I'm sure we would then to go on to learn more in spirit world, in love and light, before we can return in a new life if that's what we choose to do. It takes courage to live, but that's what we are here for. Some decide to do this act because they are not well and at that particular time and are stressed, trying to cope with difficult situations. and maybe not seeing a way out of the problems. In the spirit world that is why the lion, I believe, would sit side by side with the lamb, we are all protected. If they find the strength and courage to live on, they will get through their problems, either way each individual would be helped by Spirit.

Many people knowing they are going to die, have time to prepare and put their affairs in order, arranging their own funerals in some cases, but if you have had a traumatic passing, such as a fatal accident, or if you have a very rare passing such as being murdered, they may be in shock and not realise they have passed Residual energy is that of someone who has not yet passed through into spirit world as they are still going about doing the things they liked to do whilst here on the earth plain but in another dimension in that same time, eventually and when they are ready they will go through to love and light, their guides and helpers will help them by simply showing them the way to follow the light when the time is right for them.

Do our animals go through to Spirit?

All pets and animals go through to Spirit World and usually people feel their energy after their death, when I have read for people, a bump on the chair feeling was when a spirit cat would arrive in the room and I would get very cold legs if it was a spirit dog around, reading for a person who was strongly connected to horses, I just could see in my mind's eye a horse galloping, to give me the heads up, the strangest was thing is when you get a name of the pet, as animals we know can't talk people, and the people I read for find it hard to understand, but it may be someone you loved in the family passing the information through, remember it's all though thought patterns and to receive message from a pet, is such a comforting thing and so very rewarding for the owner. Our animals are everything to us, part of the family, why would we not want them around us still. Animals here on the earth plane are very aware when Spirit people are about, have you ever seen your cat or dog suddenly sit up and stare at the door for no reason. They see spirit easily or just sense spirit when they are about. My beautiful pet called Yoda, a 13 year old large white Persian cat, would often sit in a circle with me and gaze at nothing and we as a circle group could see he definitely knew we had spirit around us. He would always sleep at the foot of our bed and stretch the full length of it, after he died I was devastated but one night I woke up and found myself saying ouch Yoda be careful as I felt him walking over me to Johns side of the bed which he often did, opening my eyes I got a quick view of a white cat jumping off the bed… it was a great comfort.

Do we sleep in Spirit?

Why would we, if we are pure energy.

Do we have sex in Spirit?

Why wouldn't we? Many people have dreams of an orgasm experience not being in any contact with another person physically.

Do we age in Spirit?

We can be any age we wish to be in Spirit, we are pure energy, with nobody we are free.

Is there hell?

Where there is good, there is also bad, after many meditations my conclusion to this is we are all accepted into the love and light some for forgiveness some to learn, but I feel there are many levels to spirit world, if you have been a very good person in your life here on the earth you can go in on learning even more, these higher realms can help you achieve angelic levels. If you have been a bad person whilst here, I feel you would still be accepted into the love and light in the same way but on a much lower level and for you there would be much to learn, and forgiveness has to be earned.

A story I was once told when talking of heaven and hell has stuck in my mind over the years, Hell as it's known is where many people sit at a round table, the table is full of wonderful food and drink, but the people are starving as their arms are strapped up straight in front of them and as they cannot bend their arms to reach their mouths to eat, they go hungry.

In heaven they also have this round table with plentiful food and drink but the people sitting at the table although in the same situation, arms outstretched and bound are not starving they are not thirsty, because when they reach out for the food then turn to their left or right, they help to feed their neighbour's and also, they are fed by them in return showing kindness and love.

18
Spirit Guides

So, what do spirit guides do? You might well ask. They are assigned to us before we are born in some cases, and help to guide and nudge us through life. Some guides will stay with you throughout your entire life, and others will pop in every now and again to help with specific areas of your life such as goals you are trying to achieve. These guides are at varying levels of consciousness themselves. Some may be highly ascended masters and others might be your average Spirit who just happens to be a master in a certain area. They may appear to have a male or female energy as a guide, though in reality they are just energy as all things in Spirit world are.

They may have been spirits who have had physical incarnations, or they might be spirits who have never taken corporeal form. You could be the only person they are guiding, or there might be a team all looking after you, with help from your deceased relatives, that's very likely. Guides are able to tune in to your energy field and they help to direct you with your earthly mission, Guides are right by your side and when needed, so you can call on them at any time.

How do they communicate well it's an intuitive insight you get, a sixth sense kicking in to maybe tell you something and get a message across such as slow down, take a breath, believe this person or beware of this individual on trust issues, they may get you to check a situation out first by that nagging doubt feeling, perhaps they might just help you make a good decision instead of a dreadful one, and stop you making a big mistake in your life, it's always good to question things when faced with different happenings in your life. How many times have you heard people say listen to what your body is telling you - go with your gut. (Yellow chakra) It's very good sound advice. Listen to that little voice in your head. Intuitive information.

Spirit guides are with us all the time just guiding us in everyday situations, holding us back or pushing us forward. For instance, you may be ready to leave the house and you cannot find your car keys and find out later that if you had left earlier, you would have been in a terrible accident on the motorway, perhaps spirits have intervened.

It would be great to think if you could just call up your spirit guides on the phone wouldn't it, and ask their advice? Well, you can, just ask in your head, there is always someone listening, and you will always be given an answer, if you are prepared to listen to your thoughts and go with your inner gut feelings, this intuition is given to all. A classic one is when you're walking down a road and you are about to pop down an alley as a shortcut, then that little voice in your head says, no stop, go the long way round.

If you don't have a clue who your guides are or who walks with you, ask in your head and watch for signs, guides usually show themselves to you at least three times in a row, once you have asked, look for the answers, it may be in the form of a picture or something that pops up in your everyday life. For example, you may feel a draw to a certain animal and on a visit to a local shop you see a picture of a beautiful tiger and your drawn to it, go home and open a magazine and there is the picture of a large tiger; turn on the television and there on the news is a story about a tiger. Dohhhhh, hello they are trying to tell you, that you may have a totem guide, (an animal Guide) A powerful animal such as a tiger as you are needing that strength in a certain situation in your life at that particular time.

In meditation you may be able to see your own spirit guides and working with them makes your connections even stronger. They may come to you in a dream state, sometimes dreams can become very lucid and bizarre, or maybe through a book you are reading, looking for connections nothing happens by coincidence. A lot of spiritual work is letting your imagination run wild, let it flow and enjoy the ride. Guides may come in many forms.

My Experience

When giving a reading for a lady at my home, she told me she was very interested in everything spiritual and said she felt very drawn to Wolves for some reason, do I have one for a guide she asked me, as a rule I never gave guides to anyone for it's for them to discover by their gut feeling not for me to tell them. I told her that if she needed to know, we could ask whilst doing her reading for confirmation by sending a sign. The reading went well and she went off quite happy, if it's right they will let you know I said waving her off. About half an hour later I heard my mobile phone ringing from the garden I ran in to answer it and soon realised this excited voice on the line was her, she sounded elated, and through this excitement she blurted out after she had left my house and as she pulled up at the road junction to let a rather large four by four pass by she turned to follow it, on the back on the wheel cover, there was a beautiful picture of a wolf that seemed (her words not mine) to look straight at her, is that my confirmation she asked, oh yes I said there is no such thing as a coincidence.

My Personal Guides

I have four main guides and many helpers that I work with, some helpers are family members or people from my past such as my dear beloved Uncle Ben and I know my Totem Guide the Alsatian dog is still with me to this day, for me seeing him at the end of the string all those years ago, was a delight now I just sense him. I knew he would keep me safe, this very large but beautiful playmate, and a welcome friend. When I got older bringing up my boys, I would feel my Nan around me a lot and in churches she would send messages through other mediums and when Dad passed the connection was instant like he always had my back. I think Mum kept to her word and is resting in peace bless her.

First Guide - My Chinese Guide

I believe he was given to me for a little wisdom. I always found it difficult to actually see him in my mind's eye and gave him many faces at first, these different versions came into my head, and I am sure in the early days I would simply overthink things, conjuring him up in my mind and created many images of how I wanted him to be, constantly asking for evidence in my head and eventually he came to me in dream state, not what I had imagined in meditation at all, but a frail bend over little man with a bright royal blue outfit and a box type hat, he had porcelain skin and very thin white hair with a long plait coming down his back and a thin but pointed long beard. I needed to get confirmation of my dream so when visiting a spiritualist church to see another medium work, I asked in my head for some evidence. I got no messages that evening, and after the medium had finished, he thanked everyone for coming and added, 'By the way. As I was working, I kept being shown chopsticks. Can anyone take this?' I raised my hand and said yes thank you, that's fine. My guide has no name but he is with me for my grounding and for knowledge and advice helping me to make sense of mediumship and for looking at things from different perspectives. To have no name for him does not matter, just knowing he's there for me is enough.

Second Guide - Ashude

Ashude is the policeman that had helped Mum and her family whilst in Rabat years before during the war, and my second guide. Mum and I talked about him lots and lots and maybe that is the connection. I had been given him many times in churches, but the name pops into my head very easily and it's usually when I need to be a little more patient and considerate. His advice and assistance seems to come into play. When we recently went into the family history on my grandmother's side there was indeed an Arab link. He appeals to the softer side of my nature. He has a calming influence on me. When he pops into my head, it's always at times when I need to calm and slow things down a bit. I sense his gentle nature and his love, it's a great feeling. I always see him dressed in white, he is immaculate and he has olive skin, and his face is soft and kind and he has a long-pointed nose, and deep dark brown eyes. Slim and slender and his hands are small but with long fingers. Ashude can always come to the front of my mind in times of upset or trouble.

Third Guide - Matoba

My third guide has been given to me for healing and strength and came to me directly with proof and evidence. I have no need to imagine anything about him I have seen him. A strong tall magnificent Zulu Warrior.

Sitting on my own one afternoon in my lounge, about 3pm, and having been to the library that day to take a book out on spiritual guides, I suppose I was very engrossed in this book, I tend to read out aloud when alone, and had been doing this for a while as with dyslexia, I find it helps me digest the information and it actually sink into my peanut brain. Out of the corner of my eye I began to get a swirl in my vision. I immediately put the book down and looked toward the garden and thought 'Oh b****r, I'm getting a migraine." The swirl was different though and I noticed it when I looked towards the area of the fireplace in the corner of the room, swirling and swirling continued, but if I looked back towards the garden, my vision was clear. The penny dropped this swirling was indeed inside the bungalow and not in my eye but actually in the lounge by the fireplace, which was by now being obscured by this swirling of colours. I know when I am getting a migraine attack, I lose my vision gradually, and many jazzy patterns appear, but this was so completely different. This swirling in the corner of the lounge continued, it became a circle and gradually got larger and larger and more of an oval in shape at one point.

I was absolutely transfixed on this and it was fascinating but a little frightening at the same time, if I am honest. It was as big as a child's hula hoop growing in size, back to the perfect circle shape it was to my amazement an opening portal, then it became taller reaching up towards the ceiling, suddenly I saw bright colour coming from within blue sky and fields of green in the background the land was flat with hills in the distance. Then appearing from within the portal was a very tall well built fully dressed Zulu Warrior, complete with grass skirt, beads round his neck holding a large spear in his right hand. I could still see a lot of green in the distance behind him and hills beyond, and he was being followed by another warrior close behind him. His hair was black and very thick and it was swirling round which prevented me from seeing his face clearly. truly amazing albeit a little scary.

I looked down to see his bare feet and there were grass bands around his ankles and his knees were covered, the grass skirt was thick and beige in colour also as I looked up towards him, he took a step towards me to come out of the vortex that he had created, his hair still looked quite magnificent swirling around. I suppose my fright took hold, and I froze closing my eyes tightly, as at this point, I could not move a sort of paralysis took over me and as I closed my eyes tight literally squeezing them shut everything went completely black in my inner vision and then one by one all the chakras came to me in order out of the darkness in my mind from the bottom base red to the top white, the fear went instantly as when the sequence of these chakras finished I opened my eyes, I found he had gone, the room was as it had been before, all I felt was amazement, I knew instantly who he was, my Healing Guide. There was no doubt in my mind whatsoever, no fear either, just a feeling that people will never believe me and a sense of numbness and shock I suppose, that I had experienced such a spiritual event. I walked round the bungalow in a complete daze.

The name Matoba came into my head, but not on that day, only when I asked in my head a few days later. Not being sure what to do after having just had this amazing experience I did what most of us do. I made a cup of tea. I just kept thinking who would understand or believe me. How can you ring a friend and say a Zulu warrior has just stepped out of a vortex in my lounge? When John came home, about 5.30 that evening, I could not hold it in any longer. I told him straight away and to be fair he just listened, he did make a joke of it, but then it lightened the conversation by saying, well if I disappear come and look for me, I may have been sucked into the vortex in the lounge, but that was ok, we both laughed and I felt good at having told someone. It did happen, and it was very real and I shall remember it for the rest of my life. I was not asleep and I was not imagining it. Whenever I gave hands on healing after that or sent absent healing to anyone, I knew he would help me, it was such a comfort. Healing Guilds can come to us in many forms, mine I knew was just magnificent.

My Fourth Guide is an Indian Guide

At one of my Circle groups, at home one evening, we were all asking for our guides to come forward. Many in the group did not know who their guides were, so as a group we asked to be given names and to see faces of our guides. It was a good practice, as all six of us had opened up to Spirit together and were energised by one another. I ran a few Circles from home, usually on a Thursday evening. John would be out himself at his Masonic meetings, so I had the house to myself apart from Yoda, my beautiful Persian cat who loved to join in and sit in the middle of the circle. Working at home relaxes me totally and you do get good results. There were usually six to eight people in a group at any one time and we all became good friends and totally at ease with one another. After asking for guides to come forward, I got the name in my head of White Feather. I had been told by a lot of Mediums that they felt a Native American Indian Guide around me and I remember thinking how wonderful it would be to have one, as when I have read about them, I realised many of their beliefs are mine. After that evening I did find that actual white feathers would appear around the bungalow. I know we all have to walk before we can run, but I was getting increasingly frustrated at not being able to put a face to the name and as white feathers are usually associated with Angels being around, I thought I had got it wrong. These white feathers would appear in odd places too, a beautiful spider's web appeared over my conservatory roof and in the centre, you could see a beautiful large white feather. Good confirmation I thought, however I started to throw my toys out of the pram and went through the bungalow ranting saying, 'Ok, so if you're my spirit guide show yourself'; I remember saying a naughty word in sheer frustration.

That afternoon doing the housework, I started as usual in the small porch, as I would usually work my way backwards through the bungalow starting with the porch it had a long glass table in there with ironwork legs with a matching mirror above it, so I gave it a spray and wiped it in the usual way and continued on. I finished the house work and heard the postman drop some mail in. Going back to the porch I saw the mirror was looking almost cloudy again, thinking the cloth may have had something on it I went to fetch a clean one with just hot water to wipe it, but the next time I looked at that mirror it had changed again, so much so, I was compelled to take a photo of the shapes that were forming in it, the cloudy appearance was a haze and there was a rod type line going across one corner, then on taking another photo and another I saw a large white feather was forming in the top right-hand corner. This is when things started to get a little bizarre, a silhouette of a face side view came into view, wow another special moment. Looking back at me was my Indian guide called White Feather, letting me see his face. It was a gradual process but stayed for weeks and he would reappear for me if I simply asked in my head.

As I was taking the sequence of photos, I could not believe my eyes. I had asked my Spirit guide, White Feather, to come forward and here he was in all his glory. A long slender face, that was handsome yet gentle. I would thank him and just enjoy his blessing.

I think you will agree it's really amazing and a lot of visitors who came to the house saw him at that time so it was not just me, none were frightened by the experience at all, but like me they felt very, very privileged that he appeared and stayed for a while. You will see for yourself in the pictures below very clear evidence, a bright rod shape appears under his face, I believe this to be a sort of orb, a travelling vessel if you like. I now could not only tell people about this spirit guide of mine I could show them the evidence. The rod I believe is his transportation as it would become smaller when his face appeared stronger and clearer, and when his face started to fade it would become thicker and longer My mirror in my porch had become a portal. He is with me a lot and he is with be for strength and love and gives me a lot of very spiritual knowing's. and above all courage.

1. In the top right-hand corner, I saw smudging that resembled an eye, nose and feather

2. The smudging started to develop into a face

3. I noticed a line like a rod and the face seemed to appear

*4. The rod started to appear again
as he was fading*

*5. As the rod became stronger
the feather was clearer*

6. *His image is starting to fade*

7. Last image taken before it started to fade after 5 weeks

Spiritual Totem Guides

Animal Spirit Guides are called Totem Guides they help, guide and protect you and educate you and heal you through some of life's difficult journeys. We know in times of troubles how comforting pets can be, just being there for us giving unconditional love.

To the Native American Indians, Totem Guides are very important in their spiritual beliefs; each individual is associated with at least nine different animals through their life's pattern, as their guides and helpers. Usually in dream state these guides make themselves known to you at some point.

Native American Indians Zodiac signs are:

Otter	Jan 20 - Feb 18.
Wolf	Feb 19 - March 20.
Falcon	March 21 - April 19
Beaver	April 20 - May 20
Deer	May 21- June 20
Woodpecker	Jun 21- July 21
Salmon	July 22 - August 21
Raven	September 22 - October 22
Snake	October 23rd - November 22
Owl	November 23 – December 21
Goose	December 22 – January 19

In Chinese astrology there are 12 Chinese zodiac signs:

Rat
Ox
Tiger
Rabbit
Dragon
Snake
Horse
Goat
Monkey
Rooster
Dog
Pig

The western zodiac which is made up of 12 constellations:

Aries   Ram
Taurus   Bull
Gemini   Twins
Cancer   Crab
Leo   Lion
Virgo   Virgin
Libra   Scales
Scorpio   Scorpion
Sagittarius   Centaur
Capricorn   Sea Goat
Aquarius   Water Bearer
Pisces   Fish

It is said that a spiritual totem guide watches over you, they may not stay with you all the time depending on your life's pattern, different guides and helpers will be with you constantly. They come in when you are at a crossroads in your life. You may have several animal totem guides helping along the way in your life, although most people have only one or two that are front and foremost in what you do. I believe Mythical Animals should also be recognised for strength as they help also coming to us with wisdom, insight, and messages and specific energy imprints, they come to you in dream state usually animals such as:

Phoenix
Unicorn
Mermaid
Dragon
Griffin
Yeti
Kelpie
Kraken
Basilisk
Centaur
Werewolf
Sphinx
Gremlin
Hydra
Hippogriff

Loch Ness Monster
Harpy
The Minotaur

We should all pay attention to dreams as these have special meanings spiritually, but that would be another book as there is so much to learn about them. To recognise your personal animal connections simply make a note in a journal or diary, pay attention to the details that come to you in dreams and literally see what seems to cross your path in everyday life. Quite often they might just be animals you like or are drawn to on an emotional level, but I feel you will get an inner sense if they are your Totem Guide.

Many animals here on the earth mourn their dead, such as primates:

Baboons
Macaques
Gorillas and Elephants and some birds

Groups of birds known as corvids including crows, ravens, magpies and rooks - have been observed holding improvised "funerals" for deceased relatives. Elephants when a family member dies are lost, or become ill themselves, it affects the whole animal family as they effectively support one another in the grieving process within the surviving pack members allowing the pack family to move forward. Animals do display grief in a manner similar to humans. Even dolphins act so differently when one has passed to Spirit.

Some animals are said to be omens of death such as crows, vultures and bats - OK so they come out only at night, and when the night is at its blackest, perhaps that is why we wear black when someone passes over, they are simply nocturnal, but they can also represent transformation and renewal spiritually for me. Animals bring so much joy into our lives why would they not be spiritual. A dove released at a funeral symbolises that of peace and hope and freedom, it's very cathartic to some also symbolising letting go.

So, what can our animals give us?

Here are some examples:

Bear	To give us strength and solitude and focus.
Bee	Teaches us Diligence, Productivity.
Butterfly	Helps with Change, Love, Transformation.
Buffalo	Confidence and how to achieve goals.
Cat	Magic and Mystery, Clear perception, Agility.
Cow	Nurturing and Growth.
Dog	Loyalty, Unconditional Love.
Dolphin	Communication, Harmony, Trust.
Dragon	Fertility, Wisdom.
Lion	How to find joy in all circumstances; power animals.
Owl	Teaches Magic, Wisdom.
Panther	Valour, Grace, Swift action Power animal.
Rabbit	For Love, Vigilance, Fertility.
Ram	Adventure and Power.
Sheep	Purification through forgiveness.
Squirrel	Trust, Preparedness.
Tiger	Power animal for Passion, Sexual energy.
Whale	Provision, Creation, Awakening.
Wolf	For Freedom of Spirit, Discipline, Loyalty.
Dragon	Dragon is the most powerful of all Spirit Animals, offering us the energy of Ancient Magic and Primal.

My Spirit Animal is an Alsatian Dog. I have had this beautiful dog which has been a protector since birth, I believe, and I can always depend on him to be there when I feel down or vulnerable. I get such cold legs when he is near and feel a sort of draft go past me in a room, that's how I know he is about. He is strong, he is faithful and gives me comfort.

Big Cats Tigers and Lions

These Big cats come into my dream state usually and in these dreams, they are walking around the building that I am inside. I never feel afraid of them, just a little anxious, when they are around the bungalow. I see them walking around the outside, never inside and always walking slowly. I feel they are protectors and tell me to be wary of certain situations.

Horses

I have never had a horse, but have ridden when younger, and I do have an affection for them, I love pictures and paintings of them and just seeing them in a film on TV fills me with love for them, and they gladden my heart, to me they are a sign of strength, pride and love. They can live up to thirty years, many have worked alongside man, but when of a certain age, like us I think they fully deserve an early retirement and an easier life.

Robins

Oh, the beautiful Robin, these are tough little birds and people often think of departed loved ones when they see a Robin. They can comfort you and are said to be messengers, as Angels are, they are tough and stand no nonsense. They are very territorial and live about only a year, to me that is why they are so special. So, think about what animal you are drawn to and why.

The Gatekeeper

The Gatekeeper or Doorkeeper as some like them to be known, is very special and does a very important job for you and you only. They are not emotionally involved with you but have a very significant job to do, which is always to protect your consciousness, as that is the part that we take with us when we pass to spirit world. I always refer to my Gatekeeper as the protector of my consciousness.

Your communication with the Gatekeeper is only possible if it's what you yourself want to do. They are protective and they do their job by staying close, just to protect you against dark energies and bad spirits. Finding some sort of harmony with your Gatekeeper is what you need to achieve. They are on a much higher vibration. All communication with your Gatekeeper depends on your Mind Body and Spirit being willing to acknowledge them and always thank them for their protection when opening and closing to Spirit.

When you are sharing your thoughts, hopes and dream and aspirations, even problems, with spirit, you can do it anything just by sending them the thoughts from your mind, and when you are meditating and start to open your chakras to talk to spirit, its then that you ask your gatekeeper to stand aside, allowing the contact to flow between you and those in spirit world. When you have finished and closed all your chakras again your next request is to ask the gatekeeper to once more step back and continue the protection. Then and then only, can you find the right communication or vibration for contact with them. Once you have gained that level of understanding, you will feel safe and comfortable. Before I would work on the platform, I would ask my Gatekeeper to step aside leaving the door open to Spirit world and when I finished, I would simply ask them to come forward and continue with the protection, simply asking in thought patterns. Being that our Gatekeeper is not on an emotional level they just do their job, which is protecting our consciousness.

My Experience

One evening I went to bed early and sat up reading for a while waiting for John to come home from a meeting, it was about 10pm, there was just a side light on which I turned off and before settling down I asked in my head for my Gatekeeper to protect me always, and to keep me in love and light, suddenly it was as though someone had placed a light bulb over my head, I was in a sort of void hearing beautiful music, music that I had never heard before, magical, but almost like an ice cream van music but very soft and spiritual. I felt this light get stronger and stronger and a wonderful feeling of peace came over me, like nothing else mattered, just me, the music and the light. I am not sure how long it lasted, it may have been a matter of seconds but in that time, I was transfixed, in an overwhelming feeling of pure love. Then it stopped, and I could not get to sleep after having that experience. When John came home literally moments later, I did tell him, but how do you explain such a feeling of pure love. Johns use to me coming out with weird and wonderful happenings, never to judge or mock me about it, he would just listen and put it down to another spiritual adventure of mine, for which I was so grateful as when something happens in life like that, you do need to off load and talk to someone about it, he would listen.

I feel it is necessary to say that if you wish to become a medium or just connect to Spirit with a genuine desire, you will indeed have these sorts of things happen to you, and for you to find out who your spirit guides are, will help find the answers which is very important. In mediumship it is vital to achieve these personal connections to Spirit and without them it may not be possible to have any proper connections at all.

To get on the correct vibration, linking between this world and that of Spirit the key is total belief. The Gatekeeper is the protector who gives permissions for this to happen in a safe way, simply by stepping aside and then returning when you have finished, your guides then come forward and bring with them anyone who wishes to communicate with you, a sort of go-between from their side and ours, their concern is always our wellbeing. I am not afraid to speak out about these happenings as I am sure I cannot be the only one experiencing these wonderful events and whatever you think about me, I don't worry as I know it's real. If you are unable to imagine your guides by not being able to visualise then, don't worry they will find a way to show themselves, stick with it, because that inner gut feeling will kick in to let you know when they are about.

19
Angels

I personally work with Archangel Michael, and Archangel Chamuel and Archangel Haniel. Archangel Chamuel can help with your spiritual soulmate relationships and is associated with pure love, and will settle you if ever you are feeling in deep sorrow about a situation. Archangel Chamuel will help you renew and give you upliftment in certain situations such as in times of divorce or separations, when you feel your heart has hardened in certain relationships, call upon Chamuel to help. When you feel full of despair, or you become depressed and things seem hopeless, this Angel will give you a reason and a purpose to continue on.

The Archangel Michael is one of the strongest Archangels to have with you for when Satan was an angel and turned bad along with about a third of the angels in the Kingdom of Heaven, as we know it. It was Archangel Michael that kicked Satan out together with his followers that had turned against heaven and fallen from grace, hence the term fallen angels. The Angels that chose to follow Satin are on the dark side in devil worship, banished by Archangel Michael who is a warrior whose light triumphs over the darkness or any type of negativity, he stands, with a sword in hand ready to protect anything that is negative around us in our own energy field, he is saying to us you are safe whilst he protects us against the dark side. Archangel Michael will provide empowerment and take us on to the next challenge in life. If you are in a stressed or in a painful situation, call upon him to help.

My Experience

I remember calling upon him when my niece was getting married. We had travelled down to Lewis in Sussex and on the Friday afternoon ahead of the wedding it was raining and looked pretty wet and dull. My niece wanted to get married outside in the gardens of a hotel, instead it was all looking as if we would be inside, with dark overcast skies. Walking down Lewis High Street that Friday afternoon, I spotted a church with a large Archangel Michael statue outside the building. I asked John if we could pop in for a moment. I sat very quietly and asked Archangel Michael for a good day, a Sun filled day. I came out of that church with an ok feeling. The next day was wonderful. The rain had stopped, the grass dried out and the wedding took place as arranged, outside. I felt that Archangel Michael had given me that reassurance, and the sun shone.

Archangel Haniel is the angel that helps you with your energy levels and with whatever you desire, just ask in your head let Archangel Haniel know your intentions, and this Angel is associated with Moon Stones, as the moon's energy can make you feel charged with renewed different energies and emotions at times, Archangel Haniel encourages you to stop looking for joy on the outside and to be happy from within. You can call upon this angel to get you back on track and ask to be filled with joy. Archangel Haniel is also associated with the colours blue and white and turquoise as energy auras.

The function of an angel is to provide us with our spiritual and emotional needs. They are Messengers that take care of us when needed, we can call upon them in the same way we call upon our Guides and helpers. Angels are neither male nor female, but are often referred to as he or she, however they are in fact just energy. When they do appear, they present themselves to us in a way that we are comfortable with so as not to frighten us. Some are seen as great balls of light, some as just colour or sparks of energy or certain smells can be linked when they are around. As we are born with free will, Angels are not permitted to interfere with our life's pattern unless we ask them to. You can ask them anything and talk to them about anything all from our thoughts in our heads. They are from a very high Realm; Spirit Guides are like guardian angels but have never been angels themselves. We can sometimes see Angels in dream state, and when a white feather is found, it's said it's a sign of an angel, usually where a white feather would not normally be. Tingling above the head or a rush of warmth, are also clear signs of angels being present. Animals see spiritual things all the time, tiny babies also, have you ever noticed when changing a nappy of a baby they often look past you at spirit, and they start smiling at something above or around you, music in your ear and finding coins in odd places are also signs, some people find synchronicities of number occur also a sign angel are present.

Archangel Michael

I like to use Angel cards for advice and communication, especially when I am doing readings on a regular basis. At the end of a session the angel cards were presented to people and they would be asked to pull three from the pack more often than not they would confirm a reading.

When using Angel cards, try to use them in a way that is a routine, always asking in your head the questions you need answering, then by picking three cards in the same sort of format each time, you can receive the answers. I would shuffle them the same way each time and pick three and it's not always past, present and future – it is a pattern of cards that will give you a picture of what's happening in your life at that particular time as you instinctively go for them in the right order. When you go to purchase a pack of cards it is best not to let anyone pick them for you, just pick the one pack that you are personally drawn to, handle them a lot and make them yours. Store them by your bedside table if it's close or somewhere that is nearby. When first opening a new pack, place them on your chest and ask for them to work for you, make them yours. Angels work in pure love and light and energy and are of a much higher realm. Crystals can be placed next to your cards in storage for even more energy. Find the method that's right for you, make it your format and stick to it each time.

My Experiences

My own personal experience with angels was when I was first getting into the subject of spiritualism and asking so many questions in my head. It was on an occasion, again at home, sitting late one night meditating in the lounge, three sparks jumped across my rather large six foot long coffee table, then a ball of light appeared, it was like someone had turned on a very bright spot light in the room it was dazzling, you could not look directly at it for its glare, almost like staring into the Sun. I think the Angles were just answering questions from my head as to yes, we are here, we do exist, a confirmation if you like, for me, was I scared? Not at all. I would say it was another amazing experience. No profound message was given, I just had an overwhelming feeling of peace in my heart. Confirmation that they exist is what I had asked for.

One day a gentleman phoned me at home, just out of the blue I had never met him but he had heard I was a medium, question for you he said, 'Do Angels exist?' Then he went on to tell me his story of how he was travelling back quite late at night by train and realised he had lost his wallet. He went on to tell me that he had gotten into a bit of a panic, as he had no way of paying to get home once he got off the train and it was a dark winter's evening, he felt very anxious and was getting himself into a state. He sounded in his late sixties or maybe early seventies, over the phone. He went on to explain how the train had only one stop to go before he got off, the doors opened and a rather tall gentleman got on the train whilst it stood still at the station, his hair was long and covered most of his face and he must have been over six feet tall, standing there in a long heavy black wool coat he said he also noticed he had large heavy boots on, there were no other people in the carriage that evening. He then went on to tell me he was not afraid of him and as he approached, he heard him say that he was not to worry and to his amazement he cupped his hands in his and said you will be fine, and turned to walk back off the train into the darkness'. The gentleman on the phone then went on to explain to me that after the train door had closed he was once again alone in the carriage, and as he looked down he saw in his hands enough money to get a taxi home. 'Do you think he was an angel?' He said to me, 'You're a medium, you must know about these things.; 'Yes', I said without hesitation, 'I think he was an Angel sent to help you in your hour of need.', He thanked me for listening and hung up, he did not want to leave his name, as he kept saying people would think him crazy. I tried to explain how these things often happen to people, especially when they are frightened or scared. I think he needed to make sense of it in his head - poor man. At that time, I was a fledgling medium and well into my spiritual journey and had done a lot of readings for people and visited a lot of church services and psychic fairs. I was very greedy for more knowledge and experiences, all the time, it was like a vocation to me. I was loving my new found interest as well as the wonderful people that I communicated with telling me of these sort of experiences and it just confirmed my beliefs.

To start to do this work, or indeed to start opening to Spirit you need to be prepared to put in the time in and also have an open mind and heart, you don't have to be angelic yourself, you are human and we all have our failings, but you do need to do it with a little knowledge, so that you can form a base from which you can build on and always stay protected.

I am going to write about some other subjects to help you on your way, and help your understanding of how they all are interconnected. When you have decided what works for you best, you can see life very differently, and then just go with the flow.

Looking at these different subjects, some of which I am sure you may have heard of, I hope it will help you form your own opinion. I must stress I am no expert on anything. It will be my take on things, my experiences. We all have to start somewhere and I hope it gives you food for thought. When I decided to retire in 2019 I laid out my cards for help and advice.

First card - Career Transition, it told me my life purpose is triggering a blessed career change

Second card -Teaching and Learning telling me to keep an open mind and then teach others

Third Card – Creative Writing write down your thoughts
Hence the book

Runes

The earliest runic inscriptions date back from 150AD, and are particularly common in what is now Denmark, Northern Germany and Southern Sweden.

The word 'rune' itself simply means mystery, whisper or secret. Runes can be made of various materials, but are most commonly made of wood or stone, and feature symbols from the runic alphabet on them. Runes developed in areas populated by Germanic tribes, probably inspired by the Latin alphabet of the Romans. If you use Angel Cards or Runes to connect with spirit it's all about getting information. The Native American Indians would use Beaver tail bones, to get their connections to Spirit.

Tea leaf reading was very popular at one time, it's just the same, draining the tea cup then turning the cup and seeing what leaves are left inside the cup, to a good visionary medium, picture will form and they can get the gut feelings about things and then receive the interpretation of the messages, which will be given to them with help from guides and helpers direct from Spirit, reading teacups is not done much now thanks to the bags. I did this once in a workshop and saw a Scottie dog, and the lady I read for had just had hers put to sleep, I know it works.

Clear clarification in your mind, allowing a reading to flow for when you are translating and explaining and giving meanings is very important aided by Crystals, Runes, Tea leaves, Bone fragments or simply by an item from the sitter can work well for you.

Let's start getting connected.

20
Chakras and Auras

You have probably heard the word Chakra many times, it is a word meaning wheel or vortex, whenever people talk of them, they are usually referring to the seven energies which are at the centre of our being, our inner consciousness and our energy fields within our own body which help to create our Aura. They are simply pumps and valves and their job is to control the energy flows through our inner body for our wellbeing.

How we react to certain situations and how we start to master these feelings for ourselves depends on us controlling a lot of what is happening within our own minds and bodies. Medical conditions can unbalance us at times, as well as stressful situations in the workplace or at home, so before making any important decisions about the everyday stuff, or indeed life changing situations for future plans we need to be balanced and in control of our own thoughts and minds, getting rid of any anxiety.

Chakras are our filters if you like, we are able to have cut off points, it's our body and we can control it, which enables us to be more at one with ourselves. Chakras are far denser than the Aura but not as dense as the physical body.

Each of the seven Chakras are connected to the seven glands and the nervous system, each Chakra has a job to do, all our senses and our body awareness is based around these. I will tell you what colours they are and what jobs they do within us, and make it as simple as possible. Knowing your own body and knowing what Chakras do, can be a wonderful thing as you start to gradually get more control over your own wellbeing. Stress, tension and anxiety can then be controlled, as many of us know stress and tension can transform into physical pain for many of us, and illnesses sometimes get exaggerated, but this can be self-corrected for simple complaints quite easily.

One example is if you are sitting in a waiting room before going into a situation where you may feel uncomfortable, such as the dentist or a job interview, the stress of it can bring on a headache, a tummy ache, a feeling you want to be sick, and even a fear or dread, which affects your nervous system. Just a simple mind over matter exercise of going through your chakras in your head and balancing them can help enormously. Telling your inner self to calm down, finding whatever works best for you, taking control of your body and giving self-help, taking that inner journey to a happy place receiving a feel-good experience.

Communicating your thoughts to these areas can indeed take away the stress so you may relax the nerves and stop the anxiety. Trust in your ability to change things from within. Ok, so we are getting into our own head space and making sure that you are in control and then anything is possible, we can relax, calm and proceed. Learning your Chakras and understanding what they do will help you enormously. The chakras extend outward from our inner core, in our physical bodies. Most of the chakras extend forward and backward, as a spinning cone-shaped vortex of energy. The Red Root Chakra extends downward, connecting us to the earth while "grounding" us. The Crown Chakra extends upward to our higher self and the spiritual planes, connecting us to the spiritual awareness.

As we start going through our Chakras, we always begin with the Red Root Chakra so we are grounded.

When we have learnt where they are, we can then begin to meditate and start opening to Spirit. It's best to keep your feet flat on the floor, imagining large roots going into the floor that way, make sure you're comfortable in a chair and well grounded. Learning to open and close the Chakras leads to receiving the key to enlightenment and when eventually opening to Spirit you will find the connection with your consciousness and the ultimate aim of Ascension.

Sitting in a chair to do this breathing exercise correctly as it is paramount, take four breaths in through the nose, hold for a second and then release the breath slowly to the count of four, out through your mouth you are in fact breathing in the good, then breathing out the bad. Do this three times you should feel your shoulders go down on each breath out, and you will begin to relax.

RED   This is called our base Chakra, when meditating or opening to Spirit we always start with this area, it is the base of the spine, area of the bladder kidneys, hips and legs and your sexual organs. Your root chakra is responsible for your sense of security and stability and grounding.

ORANGE Called the Sacral chakra, this relates to the lower abdomen, the uterus, large bowel prostate, ovaries and testes.

YELLOW This is referred to as the Solar Plexus which is just below the ribs in the human body, related to the liver, spleen, stomach and the small intestines and the pancreas area. Your gut, and where we get our gut feelings from.

GREEN This is the heart area at the centre of our chest, breasts and the thymus gland.

BLUE This relates to the throat area and is known as our communication Chakra, the throat, the lungs and the thyroid gland.

BROWN This is around the eyebrow area and forehead, in the third eye zone and sinuses, around the Pituitary gland.

WHITE The Crown Chakra, this is the top of your head and the one that is opened when wanting to communicate with Spirit, the gateway to Spirit World and the receiver. When doing a normal meditation it can be kept closed.

These seven chakras are the main energy centres of the body. When people talk about "unblocking" their chakras, this can be done once the chakras are open, energy can then run through you freely, and harmony exists between the physical body, mind, and Spirit.

Opening and closing these chakras becomes an automatic happening for you, and if indeed you decide you are ready to contact spirit, always say your protection prayer first and ask your Gatekeeper to stand aside, it is then ok to go forward and once the white Crown Chakra is open you can connect to spirit world.

When having a small meditation or simply clearing your chakras there is not always the need to open the white top crown chakra if you are just aligning yourself, we only do this when wanting to open to spirit. We can however make sure our Chakras are spinning and balanced in the proper way. In all your meditations visualisations kicks in, you can actually see in your mind's eye what you want to achieve. Chakras are in simple terms pumps and valves to be kept free, balanced and flowing this will in turn keep the body engine happy and working as it should. Your central core is strengthened.

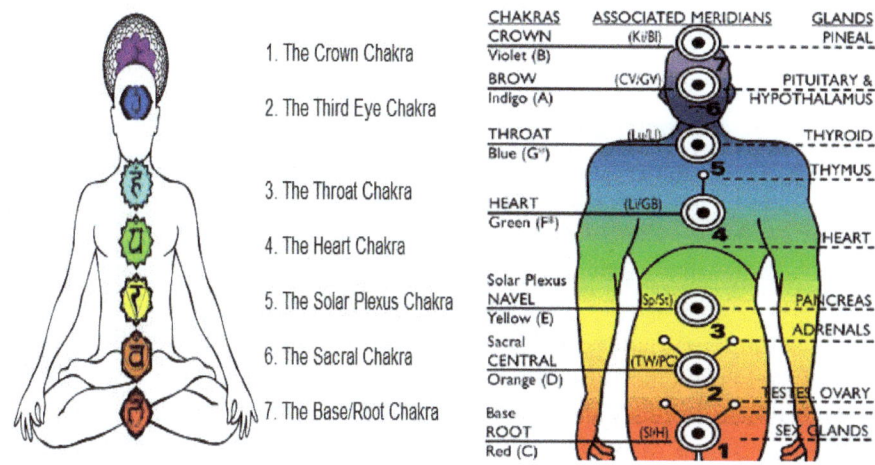

My Experience

For myself to balance my Chakras, when I am feeling out of sorts or not in tune with myself, I start by giving myself ten minutes sitting in a chair and imagine roots going down from my feet into the ground then starting at the base Red Chakra I imagine a large set of red scales you know the old-fashioned type, they are slightly unbalanced then I place some white angel feather on the unbalanced side and even it up till perfectly level. Continuing to do this all the way up I would next imagine a large pair of orange scales and go through the same process, Then Yellow, Green, Blue and Brown and White scales. It is a simple exercise you can do in your head to balance yourself and make your central core feel better, again visualisation is key imagining those scales. It is for your own wellbeing; you are putting everything in alignment again. Do it when you have time, not in a rush for better results. It can take as long as you like or can do it in 10 minutes easily. Power of suggestion, if you like you are asking your own body to follow your rules. Remember the Brown Chakra is the third eye.

If you find scales difficult to imagine then see a workman's spirit level painted red and see the bubble in the middle, showing you that its balance is straight and level. Once you feel balanced your inner central core will be stronger and in alignment, and feel the extra strength in your back. This can be done by sitting in your car at lunch times at work. It will help to chill you out on a stressful day.

Auras

In 1939, Semyon Davidovich Kirlian discovered that by placing an object directly on photographic paper, and then passing a high voltage across the object, he would obtain the image of a glowing contour surrounding the object. This process came to be known as Kirlian photography. Science could not prove that there was indeed an Aura and did not acknowledge that such energy fields existed before then. Semyon and Valentina Kirlian, two Russians accidentally discovered a camera that could capture the aura on film, and in the 1940s, the Russians began serious research into the auric field and how it relates to the physical body. By the 1970s Valentina's photography got known and completely accepted all over the world.

All living things are made up of a complex combination of atoms and molecules and energy cells which are known to generate a magnetic energy field that can be sensed, felt and even seen around the body, it's called The Aura. All living things have an Aura, plants and animals and certain objects that can hold energy.

As a medium I would sense and see this energy field around people who I read for. How many times have you said or heard it said about a person, 'Oh they have a lovely Aura about them', or 'I think I will leave them alone today as their Aura or body language is telling me to stand back'.

Semyon Davidovich Kirlian

When you are sad and unhappy your Aura is tight around your body and a lot of sensitive people will know to give you space. When you are happy your Aura can come out about twenty-five yards and people are usually drawn to you, as you are in a happy space content and have that feel good factor in your own bubble. You will see many characters in the Bible with halo auras.

It's quite possible to view The Aura of another person with the naked eye. Just stand them up against a dark wall and look slightly to the right or left of them, as you stare you will soon see the Aura that glows around them. Many times, in church when watching Medium's work up on the platform, I could clearly see this wonderful glow about them, especially around the head area.

The inner part of the Aura closest to the body is usually extended by a few inches and is a thin white light. It's believed to be the protective shield. The Aura works outwards about three or four inches further, and other colours emerge. The Aura can actually go out several feet, with up to seven layers. It's said these layers reveal the wellbeing of a person as well as saying a lot about their character and mood.

The different colours in your Aura have many meanings and interpretations - these are some I have found over years of doing spiritual work and readings.

RED	Can mean the person is anxious, or angry can be materialistic, have passionate strength, hence the saying they are seeing red when a person is angry.
PINK	Balanced individual, mother earth compassionate in nature.
WHITE	Many Different meanings, strong beliefs, easily influenced, of pure natural innocence, very spiritual person.
YELLOW	Joyous, but sometimes stubborn, generous.
GOLDEN	Divine protection, spiritual wisdom, active third eye.
MANY COLOURS	Natural healer orange Aura, powerful personality, able to control people and situations.

GREEN	Healing person, relaxed and good in company, connected with nature, can have jealousy and envy, and money growth is important.
VIOLET	Visionary and a spiritual person, good creative imaginations with strong intuition.
LAVENDER	Vivid imagination, psychic abilities ready to accomplish goals.
SILVER	Not a person to worry over finance, gives and receives.
BLUE	Emotional person, loyalty, can be a healer.
TURQUOISE	Very active person with abundant energy, a multitasking person that gets bored easily, good at organising.
BROWN	Non-believers, struggles in life, are disrespectful at times.
GREY	Calm and wise and usually an old soul that has been here many times.

My Experience

This photo of me was taken at a physics fair by a special camera showing my Aura. See how the crown Chakra is white like a skull cap, I had just finished work at that time so it was closed. I work in purple, which is said to be compassion, and the crown chakra was perfectly where it was supposed to be.

These, as I said, are my opinions and my conclusions. If you want to see what your aura is like you can simply sit in front of the mirror with a low-lit lamp with a white shade to the side of you not in front of you, as this would be too much of a glare. Then stare at yourself, first at your chin and then just to the side of your face. This takes time and practice before colours emerge.

Past Lies and Reincarnation - My take on the subject

Definition of reincarnation derived from Latin is, to take on Flesh again, which would mean taking on a physical body again, and to me it would also mean to leave one life and take on another. When I thought about it, the cells in our bodies live seven to ten years and are replaced hence we age, but our consciousness lives on. Perhaps this journey we are on now in the here and now in our present life, gives us lessons to learn which helps us move forward. In Buddhism they say there is an ever-evolving consciousness, open minds are needed to take on such meanings of life. I have come into contact with many people who I feel drawn to and comfortable with immediately and wonder if I knew them in a past life. How many times have I said to complete strangers, have we met before? I feel we really do have in our Aura hidden memories stored and thoughts hidden within it, as I believe it does hold the DNA of our life and our past lives. Open minds are essential when looking at spiritual beliefs, and respect for other people's awareness on the subject is important.

My experience

Just a recurring dream when I was a very little girl, seeing myself dressed in very tatty dirty clothes and remembering walking down to a basement area some would say a hovel and I wore a knitted shawl around my shoulders, it was cold and damp and little in the way of food, furniture, warmth or comfort. I sensed someone in there with me and then had a terrible sense of being strangled. It would wake me up in an alarming way, this dream would remain with me for some time as a child until it eventually faded, but as you can see, I remember it still quite vividly. Growing up I could not bear a tight scarf around my neck, or if anyone was mucking about in their horse play place their hands around my neck as a joke I would freak out. I have heard sometimes children have memories of things and events that they could not possibly know about, could it be just a memory from a past life? that has not been stored properly in the Aura of our being.

Dowsing

This is a technique for searching for minerals or water underground, ley lines can be detected this way and it's for seeking anything that might not be seen by the naked eye, Dowsing was done by simply using forked twigs in the olden days, and nowadays copper wires are held within copper tubes, so that they can turn easily without being influenced by the holder. These Dowsing rods react in their own way independently, then the user, the person using the dowsing rods can observe which directions they pull towards and can get a good idea of what path to walk or follow as Spirit leads them. Some use a pendulum to aid dowsing also. As with unseen influences it spins and turns. Also, the same as a Pendulum you can ask Spirit question and the rods will cross or point as an answer to the questions.

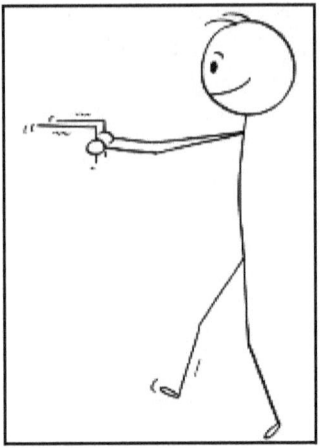

Spiritual Dowsing

Dowsing can tell you how far a person's Aura is extended if you approach someone with these copper Dowsing rods after asking them to think sad thoughts the rods cross at a point that's very close to that person, meaning the Aura is tight to them, if however, you ask them to have happy thoughts you may just take one step forward towards them and the rods will cross, telling you the Aura is wide and extended. You do not necessarily see the colours but you feel the energy. This experiment can be done with trees for example, to see where the rods will cross shows the extent of the trees Aura. It's a method that is both simple but effective. People have been finding water with forked sticks ever since the time of Moses. When you are in a search for anything using a rod, you must clear your mind and then focus on whatever it is that you are searching for. It helps to say out loud the name of the object over and over as well as visualising it in your mind. Rod divining involves a great deal of walking about and it can be a tiring method of divining. Still, it is one of the most accurate methods of all, particularly if you personally own the rod you are using. You develop a kind of communication with them, as you work with it you are attuning to its energies and it becomes one with you.

Pendulum Work

A Pendulum is a weight of whatever small object you prefer to use which is hung from a chain or cord, never use anything magnetic, as it may change the results and it has to use its own energies to answer questions you may put to it. It is a receiver or a transmitter and responds to all your personal questions.

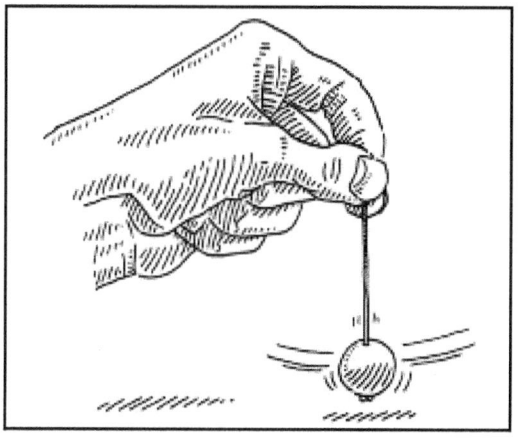

Using a pendulum. Take note of which fingers are used

Many years ago, women used this method as they would try to predict for friends who were pregnant what the gender of the child would be, simply by asking the question, and holding the pendulum over the woman's tummy you would ask, is it a boy? then is it a girl? the pendulum would swing up and down for Yes or from side to side if it was a No. They can also be used for dowsing and for healing, looking for allergies or weakness. If purchasing one for yourself remember to go for the one you are drawn to just as you would a pack of Angel cards, go with that gut feeling to see which you feel would work best for you. I was drawn to an amethyst on a silver chain, and I can clearly see faces in the stone, and it works very well.

You simply have to use your sixth sense and ask your guides and helpers to help, getting answers to the questions you ask, try to ask simple questions that need a Yes or No answer.

Before you start to use a pendulum make sure you have cleansed it and if it is a crystal then make sure you regularly charge it up in the sunshine to restore its energy, most crystals are not ideally kept in a box or a dark place they need light.

Always hold the pendulum between your thumb and index or forefinger in the hand that feels best for you, do not make the cord too long, steady it with the palm of your other hand to start, if it starts swaying let it find a level. Relax, when it finally seems to be still, start asking simple questions again with Yes or No answers should become clear. You may have to do this many times before you start to get good results, don't rush it and don't get impatient. Always before you embark on anything spiritual ask for protection first and say a 'thank you' afterwards. After all, you wouldn't ask a friend for answers or advice without saying thank you.

Start with simple things: Am I wearing a red dress? Is today a Saturday? Is the year 2023? Best not to sit next to too many electrical gadgets as they all give out their own magnetic energies. You can also find your own negative and positive side.

Try these tips

When using a pendulum, you are in fact asking Spirit to help and asking them to use their energy to give you answers to questions.

To start with, ask Spirit to show you the Yes and No movements for YES, it's usually a vertical swing, away from you and then back towards your heart, think of it as a yes nod like a nod. For a No answer, the pendulum should begin to swing sideways across your chest, liken it to someone's head going from side to side saying No.

Clearing between questions is a good thing to do, especially when you are just learning so that you know for sure you can simply stop the Pendulum and steady it with your other hand and begin again.

It's a very personal way of working. Some use pendulum work with a map for Remote Viewing, trying to plot a position as to where an item or person could be found on the map.

My Experiences

For your Pendulum you can choose whatever you want. I did some pendulum work on a friend that worked in my office years ago and predicted two daughters as she was expecting twins and it was right, but it can be a little hit and miss. The best thing is to use it every day for a while and be straight in your mind about what you want to ask before you begin.

We had a water leak in our bungalow a few years back now and much to my surprise John asked a friend to come round and do some dowsing to find it. He had just some simple copper rods held out in front of him as he walked around the bungalow when the rods and when they crossed, he knew he had found the leak. You will get use to your pendulum and it should work well for you, it does works for different people in different ways.

Enjoy it, have fun with it and make it yours.

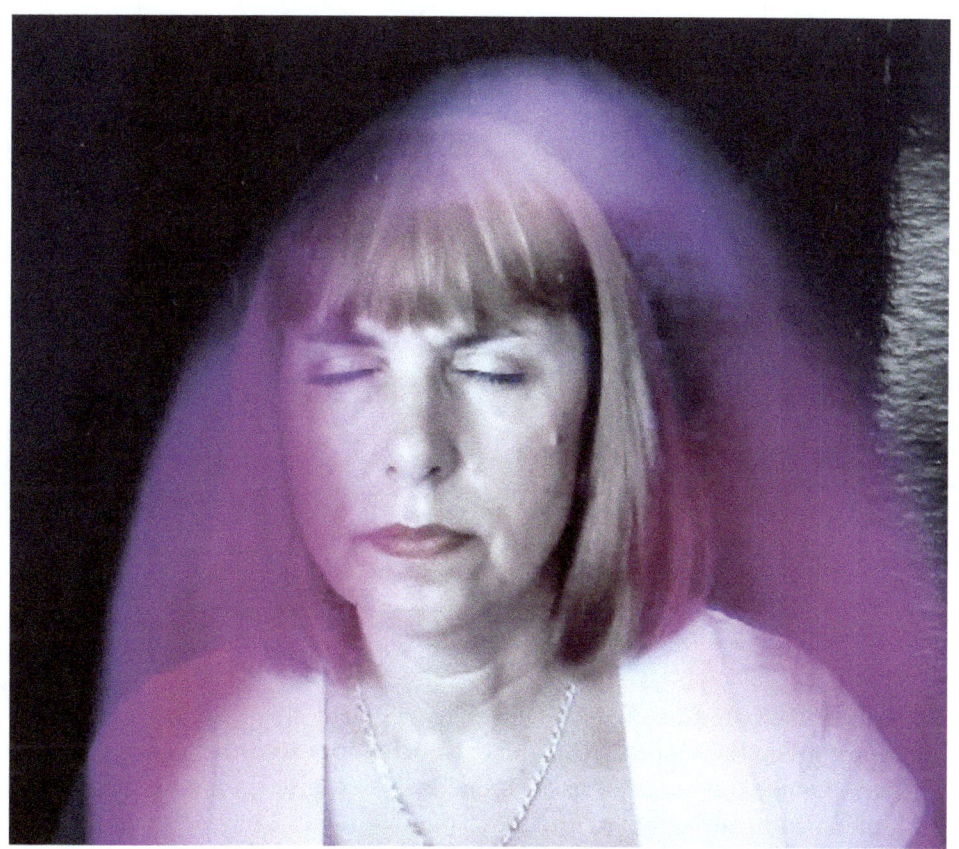

This was taken after I worked at a psychic fair showing how I work in purple and notice the crown white chakra at the top

21
Vortexes and Ley Lines

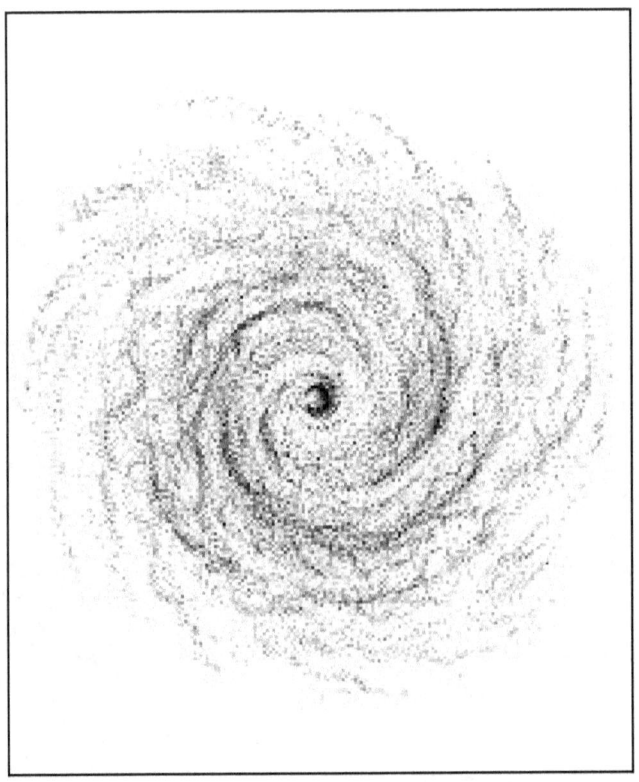

A vortex

I got interested in Vortexes after having had the experience with my spirit guide the Zulu Warrior Matoba, who appeared through a vortex in my lounge, as a spiritual experience. I wanted to find out more information about them and how they worked. I have always believed since doing spiritual work that when you die your energy, soul or Spirit whatever you wish to call it, goes through to another dimension which is actually in the spirit realm, you are not sitting on a cloud somewhere playing a harp, but right here on the earth plain in another dimension, a dimension of love and light. A Vortex is a mass of rotating, swirling energy which moves in a whirling motion, which causes a sort of vacuum such as Eddies. Here on the earth plain these are usually energies that are either electric, magnetic or with electromagnetic qualities of life force. Many are unexplainable at times but they pop up all over the earth, visible in weather patterns.

Spiritually they appear as Portals or Gateways to the spirit world. to me they are one of the answers to many of my spiritual once unanswered questions, as I do believe these portals lead to other worldly dimensions. I wonder if the thousands of people that disappear each year get caught up in them and go into another dimension? I have yet to get all the answers, but these strong concentrations of gravitational anomalies cannot be ignored.

Vortexes have been known to appear all over the world, Bermuda Triangle, Arizona, Easter Island and Egypt, some here at Stone Henge and many other sites with strong connections to Ley Lines going through them. In our own bodies Chakras are vortexes with our very own pumps and valves and they are very real.

A gentleman called Alfred Watkins taught us about Ley Lines, he found they were magnetically charged lines, routes or paths if you like, in the earth's landscape that are on a grid and they are charged with magnetic energy and where these Ley lines intercept it is said it creates very strong spiritual energy. If you are living on or near to a ley line the spiritual energies around are very strong, especially if you are near to water one of the elements. If you were to purchase a house that runs through a ley line and it's situated near a lake or stream you could indeed, have an area that holds a lot of spiritual mystical energy and activity.

Interestingly enough, time travel via what might be called a time vortex could theoretically be possible. Wormholes in space are likened to portals between two places; as it's created when two distant points in space are joined by space-time itself being bent in a higher dimension. Those who have said they have been through a wormhole vortex here on earth whilst travelling in a light aircraft have also reported to have lost time and up to an hour was unaccounted for. Makes me think when people say they have seen ghosts floating, that they are just residual energy in another dimension, but on a higher level.

Teleportation

Ok, so when I think of teleportation I think of the lovely William Shatner as James T. Kirk in the Star Trek episodes on television, and how wonderful it would be to simply pop in and out of different dimensions. Well recently researchers have indeed teleported energy across microscopic distances in two separate quantum devices, vindicating Masahiro Hotta's theory. The research leaves little room for doubt that energy teleportation is a genuine quantum phenomenon. So maybe this instantaneous travel between two locations without crossing the intervening space could one day be a reality, or may be possible for other beings in our galaxy. It has been said that we are too heavy to ever travel at the speed of light ourselves, because it would take an enormous amount of energy to move all the particles in our body, well spirit is just energy, are things people see such as BigFoot, UFOs and other strange phenomena such as spiritual full-bodied apparitions a reality of things just passing into our dimension, and returning as they appear and then simple disappear. This is what I have always believed.

Moon Patterns

The Moon, especially when it's full, has had a fascination for me ever since I was a child. Many of us believe it has powers and determines our destiny in some way, I personally think it does as without the Moon our Earth would no longer survive as a planet.

Spiritually it's been found that the Moon does indeed affect our behaviour, when at its fullest the New Moon will affect us more than the Full Moon. It is said that the Full Moon is more on the physical side and the New Moon more on the mindset. I must admit a Full Moon fills me with wellbeing, although it can affect my sleep patterns, I wake up at silly o'clock in the morning and have to go and look at the moon and feel its energy even when it's freezing cold in the garden I go out to feels its magic, or you can simply open the window or door to get the best direct view to feel its power. The New Moon seems to give fresh hope for another day and I know the importance of the gravitational pull of the Moon and Sun combined. The Moon to me has a pull on the earth, like taking in a deep breath as it pulls us towards it and then releases that energy as its breaths out, to me it is the breath of life itself and of the universe. It has as we know great power over our oceans, but it does also have these powers over our own lives in many ways, many worship the moon, and attract its energy. Spiritualists healers that use crystals for healing know that the Moon and Sun, Water and Earth can indeed be like nature's battery chargers. Crystals will absorb their energy, and so can we. The different moons have an effect on human behaviour with heightened activity in the mind. On a full moon it is a good idea to realign your Chakras.

Super Moons

These Super Moons are on the 3rd July each year also the 1st August and (also known as the Blue Moon) which is on the 31st of August and the 29th September. Since the moon's orbit around the Earth is egg-shaped, sometimes during the month-long lunar cycle the moon is at its shortest distance from Earth; other times it's farthest away. If the moon is full at the same time, it's very close to Earth, you see a supermoon. The moon had spiritual meanings each month.

January - Wolf Moon

It is the first full moon of the New year and it is known as the Wolf moon. Native Americans named this the Wolf moon because wolves howled the most during this time of the year. It is also the first full moon after the winter solstice.

February - Snow Moon

The Snow Moon gets its name from tribes in North East America because of the heavy snow and bad weather during this time of year when the frost sparkles in the sun.

March - Worm Moon

The March full moon also marks the end of the winter season and it is known as the Worm Moon, worms rise up and are spotted on fresh ground during this time of the year.

April - Pink Moon

Contrary to what people may think, the pink moon is not always Pink in colour. Many people believe that during this time, fishes from the spirit world visit the water bodies on earth to purify them. this is also known as the Sap Moon, as it marks the time when maple sap begins to flow and the annual tapping of maple trees begins. It heralded the appearance of the pink moss, or wild ground phlox, one of the first spring flowers and embraces regrowth.

May - Flower Moon

The lunar cycle was first used as an ancient way of keeping track of the time of year. There are 13 full moons in each lunar cycle, and each moon was given a name to reflect relevant seasonal events in nature. The full moon of May is called the Flower Moon because it is the time of year with the densest blooms out for all to enjoy and see.

June - Strawberry Moon

The Strawberry Moon is pretty self-explanatory. Strawberries become red and ripe during this time of the year, hence the name. The Native American Algonquin tribes that live in the north eastern United States as well as the Ojibwe, Dakota, and Lakota people's mark the ripening of "June-bearing" strawberries that are ready to be gathered.

July - Buck Moon

So called because the velvety antlers of male deer which first begin to sprout in early spring finish growing as summer peaks. They form pointed tips and harden into their final glory. The sight of their magnificent racks against the summer sky are magnificent.

August - Sturgeon Moon

The Full Moon in August is called The Sturgeon Moon because of the large number of sturgeon fish that were found in the Great Lakes in North America this time of year. The most common sturgeon in the Great Lakes is the lake sturgeon; the males have a lifespan of 55 years, while females can live up to 150 years. Surgeons can be found in abundance at this time of the year. It is also said that baby birds take their first flight around this time.

September - Harvest Moon or Corn Moon

It is known also as The Corn moon because this is the perfect time to harvest corn. The moon also rises earlier and brighter allowing farmers to work late at night. The Harvest Moon, sometimes referred to as the 'Corn Moon', is the closest full moon to the autumn equinox and is symbolic of a new beginning.

October - Hunters Moon

In ancient days, this indicated the time for hunting. Hunter's moon is mentioned in several sources as the Anglo-Saxon name for the Full Moon of October. This is the month when the game is fattened, and it is time to start preparing for the coming winter. Traditionally, this included hunting, slaughtering and preserving meats for use in the coming winter months.

November - Beaver Moon

The full moon of November is The Beaver Moon when animals like beavers start preparing their dens for the coldest winter days during this time. Since November's beaver moon is the last full moon before the winter solstice, some refer to it as the 'mourning moon' – and according to pagan traditions, is a time to let go of past troubles or grief.

December - Cold Moon

The Cold Moon in December is a mark of the arrival of winter in the Northern Hemisphere countries. The cold moon is usually observed during the Winter solstice, the time of the year when the sun is at a maximum distance from the Northern hemisphere.

Spiritualism is a balance

My Experience

I have always found that the moon does affect the way I sleep, I can be wide awake when it's time to go to bed, so when I find myself in this situation, I usually settle down make a cuppa and then do a small meditation, it's amazing the energy that's around and you can get the most wonderful colours come forward in your third eye. A school playground lady always used to say to me, that school kids were always a little wild in the playground at break times when it was a windy day, and I used to laugh, but the atmosphere around us does affect the way we are. We know our moods can be uplifted by sunshine and dulled by a grey day, The moon and its gravitational pull can affect us also, spiritually it is such an important part of our lives, go on, open the curtains and let the love and light of it shine in on a dark night. It is linked to romance and gives our planet life, what's not to like. To me when the sun goes down and the moon comes up there is a sort of balance to things.

When certain planetary events happen, they can be very spiritual as the energy of earth changes such as:

Equinox

An equinox occurs when the position of the Sun is exactly over the Equator. When this happens, the hours of daylight and the hours of darkness are about equal almost everywhere on Earth. Equinoxes take place only twice a year. In Spring and in Autumn. The name equinox derives from the word aequus meaning equal.

Solstices

The word solstice is derived from the Latin word Sol meaning sun and occurs twice a year.

A solstice is a moment in the year when the Sun's apparent path is farthest north or south from Earth's Equator. There are two solstices each year—one in December and one in June. At the solstice, the tilt of Earth toward the Sun is at a maximum angle in one hemisphere and a minimum angle in the other.

Just remember that solstices are the longest and shortest days of the year, while equinoxes occur when the day and night are equally as long.

Crystals and Stones

It is thought the first historical references to the use of crystals come from the Ancient Sumerians (4th millennium BC), who included crystals in their magic formulas. Crystals were (and are) also used for healing. Also, in traditional Chinese Medicine which dates back to at least 5000 years crystals and stone have been used. Scientists using two different age-determining techniques have shown that a tiny fragment of zircon crystal found on a sheep ranch in western Australia dates back to 4.4 billion years ago.

Crystals are formed by atoms, irons and molecules that stick together in different patterns. They are usually solid and very hard to break and can form many different shapes, depending on what atoms are mixed together and they get their colours from the natural environment where they were formed. For instance, Amethyst gets its colour from iron however it depends on how the atoms and molecules absorb the light which adds to their individuality in colour.

Mediums and Spiritual people love Crystals and I work with Amethyst stones and Rose Quartz as I am drawn to them, each stone and crystal has an energy to give out. You will feel their energy just by holding them as they seem to connect to you. They are a mineral, and some are produced by plants and animals, each is unique. Diamonds, Rubies, Sapphires and Emeralds are some of the most famous and expensive, but many are worn in everyday life for many different reasons such as Jade, Tapas Moonstones, Amber, Amethyst and Rose Quartz - too many to list.

Quartz is a common crystal that is found naturally and can also be created in Laboratories. Salt is another type of crystal. As crystals usually get their colour from the environment, you can expect to find at least 16 specific types of gems that are determined to be the most highly valued, among them are the diamonds, jade, garnet, topaz, quartz and opals.

Crystal are associated a lot with healing and like any battery they also need charging, when the sun is shining on a bright day take them out side and charge them up letting the sun's rays pour into them, also when keeping crystals indoors do not place them in a dark place in the centre of the house, always try to place them where its bright and they then can perform and do their job, place them near or in a window of a room, then placed to the edge of the house the healing can begin and you will find they work much better. If you own a Crystal, it will be unique. A musgravite crystal is one of the world's rarest gemstones, so scarce it's actually very expensive to buy. It is a gemstone believed to relieve stress, boost positive energy, and bring joy and peace of mind. Crystallographers are the scientists who study crystals.

I can clearly see faces and shapes in crystals as I do in most natural materials, they do hold a fascination for me. I feel if there was a choice of a precious diamond or a crystal that held fascination, I would choose the crystal every time.

Birthday Stones

JANUARY	Garnet
FEBRUARY	Amethyst
MARCH	Aquamarine
APRIL	Diamond
MAY	Emerald
JUNE	Pearl
JULY	Ruby
AUGUST	Peridot
SEPTEMBER	Sapphire
OCTOBER	Opal
NOVEMBER	Topaz
DECEMBER	Turquoise

22
Orbs and Rods

Many people have heard of and know the meaning of Orbs and spiritual Rods as many have also heard of ghosts and poltergeists - I would like to explain a little about them just to dispel some fears.

Everything in the universe is a vibrating energy of some sort or another and everything will vibrate on different frequencies. Orbs come in many colours and each has its own meaning. Orbs of light with their energy can often be seen more commonly in photographs or appear on videos, some people see them with their own eyes literally floating around the house. The Orbs themselves have an Aura and when captured in a photo, many people can see faces within them, it helps when we can enlarge these easily on our phones nowadays. The little floating spheres or lights are, I believe, spiritual beings and their energy. In many photos at parties, discos and weddings and family snaps, they appear maybe just floating near to stay I am still about as spirit, and to me this is very comforting, many orbs can be our spiritual protectors and loved ones, if they loved us while they were here, why would that change and I feel they would want to be around if we had a celebration. You are not to worry if you have never seen one, like I have said in this book many times. Just because you can't see it does not mean it's not there.

Orb colours

WHITE TO SILVER	High energy strength, guardian angel's protection.
PINK'S	Compassion and openness, love, affection guides.
REDS	High energy levels, creative, restless, teachers, sometimes agitated, pain or anger.
ORANGE	Comfort and healing, motivational strength and courage.
YELLOW	Inspiring, creative, cautious, pay attention to.
GOLD	Free flow, tolerance, wisdom, higher consciousness.

GREEN	Psychic development, communications of teaching.
Blue	Tranquil, healing, calming, protection, intuition.
Purple	Peace, forgiveness, spiritual development.
BROWN & BLACK	Earthbound, immature, under developed, insecure, tortured or trapped, but not in all cases.

My Experience

At Slip End Spiritual church in Luton I ran the odd spiritual workshop, I asked my dad in my head, to be round me as it is a bit daunting at times standing in front of a room full of people keeping their attention, I was trying to help them to progress on their own spiritual journeys. People are usually so eager and keen to learn, it is a joy to help them, the atmosphere was great, Phil Lewis my friend who ran the hall, took a photo of me as we were all seated in a circle and there behind me was an enormous beautiful large white orb, I feel it was my Dad, being there for me as I had asked him to be, I also got a slight whiff of tobacco, the brand he used, none of the ladies eighteen ladies in the group saw this, but the photos was evidence he was indeed with me.

Also, one night at home whilst walking across the hallway to the bathroom, it must have been about 1.30pm, I was overtaken by a large deep blue Orb, which whizzed past around me and went into the bathroom first. I was not afraid to go in, as I had been thinking about my Nan and somehow knew it was her. These orbs are indeed in my opinion concentrations of energy created by the spirit around us.

23
Signs of Spirit to Look For

When you get interested in this subject, and if you, like me, want to become a medium yourself, you start to feel differently about things and instantly know when Spirit is around you. I will list some signs for you to look out for, so you know when your sixth sense is kicking in.

It's an instinct and you know when Spirit is around you, that feeling kicks in. I would experience sudden chills around me and pockets of cold air, like you're sitting in a draft and especially if it was an animal Spirit drawing near, I would get cold legs for some reason, as a calling card for me to recognise them, my ears would get a sort of high-pitched noise from within, like a buzzed spaced-out feeling. Many nights I would wake up at silly o'clock and would have too much energy to sleep. I was breaking with normal everyday habits and becoming more aware spiritually. I knew immediately that Spirit themselves were eager to communicate with me, tingles on the top of my head and a wispy feeling around my fringe were all signs, like I was walking through cobwebs. A pulsating blink at the side of my right eye told me they are drawing close.

New ideas and new thoughts would pop into my head especially for my poetry and church addresses. Some people I know would hear gentle voices but with me personally it was though thought patterns, eating habits can change, sudden waves of emotions come in from happy to sad, anger and loneliness, all these feelings Spirit will teach you to interpret and understand, and you are shown how to deal with the different situations, and you will discover the aim is to find and accept the ultimate unconditional love they offer you.

As these different energy levels change in and around your body you become aware, not only of your outside appearance and behaviour but also what is happening on the inside of your very being. Your chakras and their energy points become vivid as you practise the opening and closing every emotion is more intense. However, none of this is all at once, it's so gentle you hardly notice at first. Be aware of how Spirit wants to communicate with you personally.

Bill, a friend that had passed over after giving me his plant, left a sign

Many old issues are brought to the front of your mind, you then have to not only face them head on, but deal with them, you cannot help others if you yourself are in a bad place. You balance things more and accept that you are not always right, as the balance is seeing things from each perspective. Seeing the other person's point of view, therefore you do not judge them, if they are bad people or unkind to you, you actually pray for them. Some would call it a cleansing of your soul; as it says a lot about you and not much about them when they are so unkind to you. The third eye when developed starts to open and you see more clearly, in some ways it's like seeing with new eyes and with more compassion. You will find your awareness is expanding, your spirituality growing, till when reading for different people you just adjust, as I have done on so many occasions, I came to realise not everything pans out the way you would like it to in life and people suffer so many setbacks along the way, and in many cases, they make the wrong decisions, as I have done myself in the past. However, I have a better understanding that we all have a life pattern and sometimes on this journey of ours we do face lots of blips along the way, who can say where any of us will be in a years' time or five years down the line, compassion is everything. If someone is persistently being unkind to you it's ok to block that person from your mind, they are only giving off bad energy anyway. Be in total control. Stand in your own power. Protect your own mind.

Things to look out for when you start getting more spiritual

Sleep patterns may change.

You start to see things differently.

Look for signs like angel feathers, butterfly's orbs and guides and helpers.

New people centre in your life for a reason.

You break free from old habits and look at the world refreshed.

Your 6th sense starts to kick in.

Your energy flows from within and becomes stronger. Strange happenings.

Emotions are heightened. Chills for no reason, or extreme heat.

An awareness of Spirit becomes second nature.

Listening to your inner gut feelings. The Yellow Chakra is stronger.

Sparks of unexplained lights in a dark room.

Voices or sounds you cannot explain. Feelings of unconditional love and compassion.

My Experience

You have to adjust to what's happening in your life, all of us are so wrapped up in everyday things, we don't stop to smell those roses anymore. Time is the greatest gift we can give to anyone, and sometimes that is learnt the hard way. Being spiritual doesn't mean you don't get angry, you don't swear, you don't let people down, you are human and everyday life is hard at times, being spiritual to me means taking time to actually take stock of things and try to get it right every day, that's all any of us can do. We learn from our mistakes and hopefully move on in a better way, it makes us stronger, more thoughtful and knowing not everyone will like you but that's fine as you will know in your own heart you did your best and you can aim to do better that's all you can do, stay tolerant positive and strong.

I was talking to a chap called Bill at a Slip End Church meeting one Tuesday night, the conversation went to gardening as he loved plants, so I started to pick his brain about one particular plant I had problems with growing, he offered to bring to the next meeting a few cuttings of his for me to pot up at home. True to his word Bill, being the very kind man that he was brought into church the following week, a few cuttings for me. Weeks later as I had not been to Slip End Church for a while, I noticed these cuttings were doing rather well. I was delighted with the results of the growth in the pots, and decided to pop along and tell Bill the results and how pleased I was with the cuttings. Before I left for the church, I took some photos on my phone to show him. Arriving at church everyone was busy as usual preparing for the service. I looked for Bill but could not see him, but then I was shocked to hear that Bill had been poorly and sadly passed to Spirit. I wish I could have told him I thought as I came away after the service feeling gutted that I had not shown him the photos and say thank you, On arriving home I popped into the back garden to water my plants, Bill was on my mind so I check my plant he had given me, and there in the pot was a beautiful white feather, I guess the message had been received and he knew.

When I decided to change my sports car for something I could actually get in and out of easily, I went to a garage in Leighton Buzzard. I was drawn to it by the name Free Spirit, the people there were excellent and always so kind, we have used them now for years. John and I walked around looking at the different cars for sale to see if anything was suitable for me, we were shown various cars but my attention was drawn to a huge Black Honda four by four, well from a tiny MG it looked massive but despite thinking I can't drive that in my head, I asked to look at it with a view to a test drive. The lovely guy there that was showing us around went to fetch the keys, when he came back he unlocked it, he said it had a massive boot so as I walked to the back of the car and opened the boot myself and saw a very large very beautiful butterfly which slowly flew out of the boot and past me, well that's a sign I said I will have it, much to his surprise and amazement of the salesman. It was indeed one of the best reliable cars I have ever owned. I called it Albert for some reason, but then I named all my cars.

Spiritual Knowings

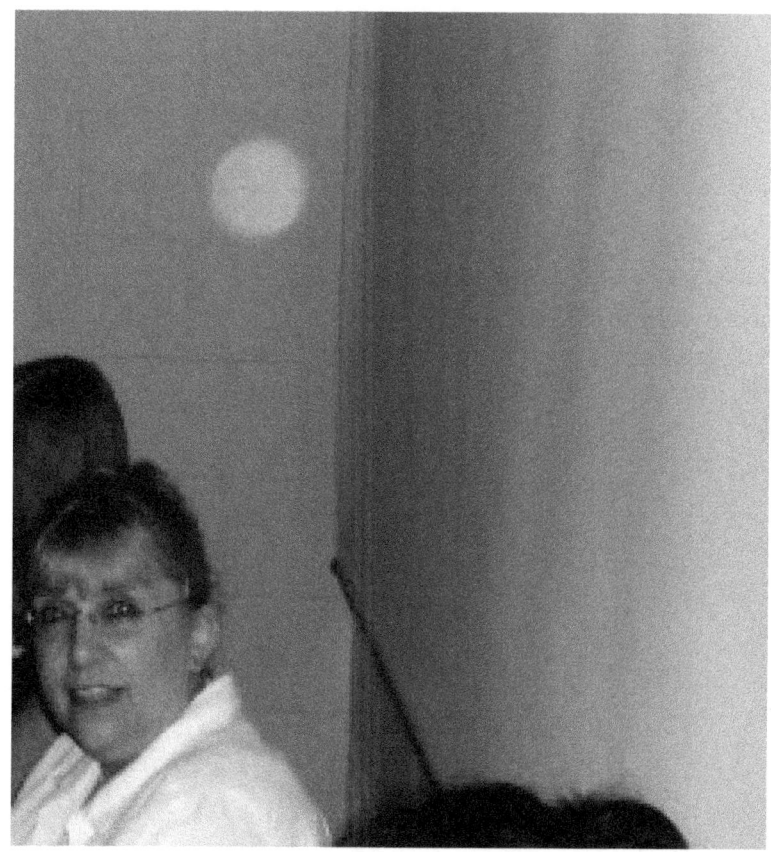

Whilst running a workshop at Slip End in Luton, Phil a dear friend took this photo of me working. I had sensed the spirit of my father around

24
The Third Eye Awakening

The third eye is exactly what it says, a third eye, how many times have you heard people say, 'Oh yes, I have seen this in my mind's eye'. It's situated in the middle of the forehead and provides a perception far beyond your ordinary sight, seeing things in many dimensions. It is used for clear sight whilst meditating and in these visions, it takes us on our amazing spiritual journeys seeing far beyond our expectations.

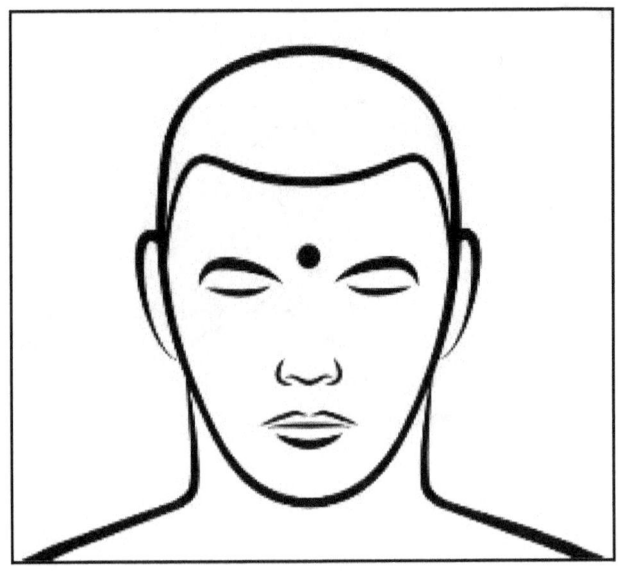

The Third Eye

It is in fact the pineal gland, its ordinary in a dormant state. It's a bit like a dried-up pea in size. and will lay dormant for most of us in our everyday life, we would not normally use it, but on becoming spiritual, or practising our meditations mediums, psychic, monks and holy men and women in prayer, with many religious beliefs all over the world will decide to open their third eye to get a greater understanding of the universe and the Spirit realms. Once the third eye is opened, meditations are sharper and visualisations into the different realms become much clearer. You are the master of your own mind and if you wish to open your third eye you can do this yourself, as you and you alone are in charge of your own consciousness.

I personally would suggest you do this under supervision, there are exercises you can do to bring this forward. Many ancient philosophers believe the third eye is the seat of your soul, and being able to use your third eye will give you the clarity you seek in your meditations and help you function and develop as you are able to see things beyond the physical.

To do this on your own without any help or instruction, is not always the best idea, I would certainly recommend you join a spiritual circle group of experienced people or have one to one session with an experienced Medium. Be aware that it can open up doors you may have wanted to keep closed, and that where there is good in love and light there can be bad in the darkness. So, protection is paramount. Stick to the rules and it will be a magical experience for you to discover.

I feel our minds are our own personal onboard computers. People may have explored all parts of the world but we still do not have a complete understanding of our own minds and what they are capable of.

When I first started to open my third eye, it was wonderful, but I did suffer some headaches to start with and also got a sort of cracking sensation in my forehead in-between my eyebrows. My head throbbed and I got a tingling sensation in the forehead itself, so if you do undertake this, take it very slowly and, as I said, maybe a good idea is to do it under supervision, in a recognised circle group they will always help, showing you the right way also to ask for protection from your guides and helpers as always.

It did, however, help me with my readings and in my meditations, things became a lot clearer. When you first start out reading for people and contacting Spirit you automatically close your eyes, well sometimes it's a good thing to keep your eyes open and look through your third eye instead of seeing your thought patterns. You cannot work on a platform at a venue with your eyes closed all the time, so get into that habit of looking through your third eye seeking the visions given to you by spirit. When it does open it's like an awakening and that calcified and dormant pineal gland opens and brings with it, wonders of the universe. Think now as you read this of say a lake surrounded by trees, keep your eyes open. The picture will be there, the third eye can bring you spiritual images in the same way.

My Experience

To practise I would sit in front of a blank wall and to my amazement, I would see a pin prick of light in the distance that would come forward and, in that light, I would see people walking backwards and forwards, a bit like the James Bond movies looking at the black silhouettes of people walking about within the white circle. You don't look with your eyes, you look with your third eye, that is the difference. When working on a platform I could clearly see pictures, images and sometimes initials and numbers, and just by asking for the images to come forward in my head it would give me great clarity for any readings.

The headaches or a crackling feeling and a slight pressure in the centre of the forehead, is all part of it and the 6th Chakra area becomes alive, it is a sensation like no other. When you experience these things, you can be sure that you are indeed doing it right and opening the third eye, the awakening as it's sometimes called. It is in fact this pineal gland that has laid dormant for so long becomes active. The throbbing and pulsing of this is normal and you may get a slight popping or crackling sensation, but it will settle down. There are certain Mantras you can chant to help. These exercises to open the third eye can be practised over three to four days in short sessions, Please No more than that.

To start you can practise a chant. Th sound this is a popular one, you need to achieve the right vibration try this by breathing in through your nose and whilst breathing out through your mouth hum the Th sound with cheeks puffed out to achieve the right vibration between your teeth.

1. Protection prayer said and in place. Sit upright in a comfortable position.
2. Feet on the floor so you're grounded. Do your 4 breaths.
3. Leave a space between your teeth and pop in the tip of your tongue.
4. Breathe in through your nose hold for the count of four.
5. Then with a little light pressure, blow out through your mouth and teeth, your cheeks should puff out slightly, to the count of four.
6. Use the voice box to sound the start of the Th sound like you're saying the word The, but you don't actually say it just releasing the vibration breath slowly.

7. Objective to puff out your cheeks and get your tongue vibrating between your teeth. It's a one-off exercise over 4 days tops.

8. Do this at least six times ONLY each day feeling the air flow through your teeth.

9. Do this once a day for about six times then just for four days NO MORE.

After this exercise, the pressure between your eyebrows begins. When people talk of soul searching, opening the third eye is usually their ultimate goal as any spiritual person will tell you, not to be afraid, but to gain a greater understanding of the universe and this in itself is very rewarding. Always with your prayer of protection in place first and always with your feet on the floor to start, give this exercise the respect it deserves. You can give yourself a mantra on a vibration word you are comfortable with. Meditations should be better and clearer so buckle up, as you enjoy the trip to Terra Incognita.

25
Healing

Everyone needs a little healing at some point in their lives and it may not be a physical thing, as people have many problems to deal with, which can affect their mental health. However, with each hurdle we have had to jump over, every struggle and problem we have had to face, actually makes us stronger people. Meeting someone for the first time, just remember you don't know them at all, they may be fighting their own battles within themselves, sometimes you don't have to ask, you can just sense it.

For all of us as individuals, every problem we face leads us to a staircase and to get over whatever problem we may face we first have to take one step at a time. The world in many ways is improving, just by recognising everyday Mental Health issues that people suffer on a day-to-day basis and being disabled in any way mentally or physically does not mean you can't do things you have always wanted to; my dyslexia was the same I was treated by some as a stupid child, now it's recognised as a condition that can be helped.

It is very true when people say, don't stress over the past, it's gone, don't worry about tomorrow it's not arrived yet, just live in the moment and enjoy each day, try to make it as happy as you can and enjoy being in the present. Life in many ways is that blank page, and if we choose to fill it with what or who makes us happy that's how it should be, above all we should not waste our time for it is the most precious gift we have been given. As Mum used to say love and you will be loved.

I was reading in a local newspaper once about a little boy aged 5 who was asked by his teacher to do a homework exercise and his was to put together a map of the world, like a jigsaw, his teacher had cut out pictures from a local newspaper, all the children had been given different pictures to take home, his dad that evening offered to help him as he said it looked a little complicated, he popped the pieces of jigsaw on a tray for his son and told the little lad to wait in the lounge with it until he had cleared up in the kitchen and then he would help him, but the little lad came back into the kitchen with it already done five minutes later, Gosh his dad was so surprised, how did you manage that he said it's quite complicated, "Oh it was so easy" said the boy, there was a picture of a man on the other side and when I put the man together the world just fell into place. Say it all…

Spiritual healing has been around a long time and there are many types of healing you can receive. It should never be used instead of receiving proper medical advice, but I must say I have known many people who have received a great deal of comfort from it when dealing with different situations in their lives.

The rules and regulations of healing are quite strict and there is a great deal of etiquette to follow. From a little girl I was taught by my mother, the laying on of hands, but now we live in a suing society and there are so many rules and regulations to adhere to, one must always check that the person you are healing is fully aware of what's happening and you always have their full permission to start giving them healing and rightly so. I would never heal anyone without asking them first and if I needed to place my hand on their head or shoulder, I would ask permission first. I did a lot of healing in churches before the services. There were codes of conduct that would have to be followed and I strongly advise any mediums out there to work within the guidelines, I had insurance and made sure I did all the right things before I even attempted it.

When laying on hands I would ask my guide Matoba and helpers to come forward and channel through me the energy needed for the healing process to begin, checking before you start healing that person for instance did not have a bad heart condition or a pacemaker fitted, as it may not be a good idea, remember as a healer you are putting energy flow into them and it can be powerful.

If your Clairsentience kicks in whilst you are healing and you sense a lump or something that Spirit is telling you or you just feel there is a problem, you would never blurt it out to the person, you would simply encourage that person to seek medical advice for a checkup to stop them worrying about a situation, as not to scare them, but to advise. If you want to be a healer, or feel you have the ability I would encourage you to do lots of workshops under supervision before attempting it, so they can learn the dos and don'ts. Just a comment such as a passing remark may put an anxious person into panic mode.

When carrying out healing myself I would get a tingling sensation from the top of my head crown chakra right through and down my arms into the hands, that is where, for me the energy and healing was channelled to, healing was received and given, often the person receiving the healing would say that the area got very warm and that it was a comfort. They also said they could see blue and many colours when they closed their eyes. You simply channel the healing from your healing guide to them.

My Experience

It's best to sit them down then ask them to go to a nice place in their minds feeling the sun shine over their heads, and let the healing commence I would usually stand behind them with my hands on their shoulders, I would have opened to Spirit first before doing this and would have also asked my door keeper to stand aside while Matoba my Zulu Warrior healing guide stepped forward, then simply by asking for the healing energy to flow through you and into them, the process begins, it will not drain your personally of your energy if done properly. We live and think inside our own heads all the time, we have to make sure it is a nice place to be.

Absent Healing

Absent healing is done by sending out prayers and asking spirit for healing for certain individuals or certain situations wherever it's needed in the world. Church Groups place people's names in their book of healing where they can be mentioned and included in the church services. On social media sites, prayers for healing can be done at certain times of the day or night to concentrate on one person or one situation. This joint healing that unites healers can be very powerful, sending out prayers in a strong united way.

I knew of a beautiful little girl. Her parents were told she had cancer and that she would need a lot of treatment to get better. I rallied round friends and the healers I knew and gave them a visualisation healing prayer for their meditations.

We imagined an ice cube, which represented her cancer and we brought the sunshine out over our heads onto this ice cube, and as the sun shone the ice would melt representing the cancer. Just simple visualisation. I am happy to say that the little girl did recover and is now a beautiful young lady, she had many hospital treatments, but with the love of her devoted parents and family, and the love of so many people, I like to think the power of prayer was a powerful tool to help and never to be underestimated.

My Experiences

I visited a very spiritual friend called Harry in hospital along with some other healers, Harry was extremely poorly, so myself along with these three other amazing friends one lady and two men we did hands on healing, Harry believed in spiritualism strongly, he ran many circle groups himself and would go to many spiritual meetings, he could barely open his eye he was so ill. I opened the window and I remember getting an urge to gather all the bad in my hands from around Harry and throw it out of the window. Where many people who had written Harry off, but we as a group of four friends thought knew he would recover, one of the guys played angelic music for him while we healed and we said prayers, he was aware of what we were doing and loved it, he did go on to make a full recovery I believe Harry was helped by the power of prayer that day and the love of his friends.

Types of Spiritual healing vary, Rekik being one and many other spiritual wellness practices, such as yoga and meditation, people turn to Reiki to manage stress, anxiety, pain, and fatigue. Feathers and burning incense can be used together with crystals and stones with strong energies, the amethyst is used a lot as a healing crystal in many cases. In short, it is a way of managing both mental and physical health. These Alternative Therapies work very well for some, but should never be replacement for a doctor's appointment.

Maybe give yourself a little healing and if you are the sort of person who finds it difficult making decisions about things, maybe, this will help you focus and make the right choices, by making the energies inside you work just for you, instead of against you achieving your aims are possible, knowing that you never walk alone, Angels, Guilds and loved ones that have passed walk with you and help. When you finally feel surrounded in love and light it is feeling like no other and it is The Knowing, being able to manage physical pain as well as mental pain, being supported by a higher realm, it is where the saying, (find your inner strength) comes from. Many achieving athletes will tell you that their head space has to be right, before a competition. We all have problems in life to deal with financially or socially but this will help us cope and before our problems lead us to more additional problems such as using drugs and drink as an aid to numb the pain, we can focus on facing our lives and dealing with things in a better way.

By accessing this free higher power within ourselves we can come to terms with the truths of our life. Filling ourselves with love is not easy, especially when some folks are so hard on us, but finding that forgiveness and understanding make us feel better. Don't be a victim, be creative in all you want to achieve, ask Spirit for what you want in life they are listening, your confidence will grow and your worth becomes apparent.

When you reach the point when you can almost hear the quiet, you are not thinking of the questions in your head space but receiving your answers from within, then and only then have you accessed your inner self. To boost your body's ability to heal in mind, body and spirit concentrate and focus on creativity as it will energise and balance you. This is all possible. The new attunement of your mind is very doable, we all have in our everyday consciousness total control and we are able to go deeper, to find the awareness of Spirit just let your imaginations fly to see into the universe.

26
The Dark Side

Where there is good, there is also bad and we should always ask for our homes and ourselves to be protected. We can do this ourselves; I visually place a gold band of protection in my mind, all around my home including my family and friends and in that thought ask for all included to be kept in love and light, it does not take a minute to do and is very effective.

Bad Spirit can drain your energy and if allowed to do so, it can also affect your home's atmosphere. If you have problems with bad energy in your home, you can yourself do something about it or ask a Medium to come and cleanse your home, but only if you should feel the need, usually it is achieved by saying prayers then the burning of white sage wafted round with a feather. Job Done. Turning that negative energy in your home into positive energy once more will do the trick. The stronger you are in your mind the better it will be to deter an unwelcome Spirit should they be menacing. They may have come in via an opened portal it's not common though, so don't panic, and don't be frightened to call it out and ask them to leave. I have never had the need to do this in my home but I do open all the windows to bring in the fresh air and waft out any negative energies most days. As buildings do store energy.

Sometimes a portal may be opened accidentally and you are unable to control what comes in or you may inadvertently bring in a bad energy that may be attached to an item such as an antique item. You have to be strong and stay in complete control. Whenever you find a portal has been opened accidentally, just make sure it's closed and blessed and you should not have any further problems. In all of these spiritual things your mind has to be strong as you are the one in charge always.

There are of course demons and bad spirits and a number of evil beings on the darker side of things, but when we show our strength, we show them who's in charge. Love does conquer in these situations and no matter how bad things get, they can be turned around, we are always under protection from our Angels and our Guides and helpers. Our inner mind has to be protected and strong at all times.

Imps who are opportunists and cause problems usually come from the ground or unprotected portals, these little demons are about, and people find they lose things or things open or close by themselves, the word Poltergeist is usually spoken with dread, as they like to bang and crash about to make themselves heard, but poltergeist is a German word meaning Ghost, we generally laugh at the word ghost, but poltergeist frightens us when it shouldn't. If things get out of hand again Specialised Mediums will help you with the problem, by cleansing the house and asking them to leave, just get in touch with your nearest spiritual church for advice.

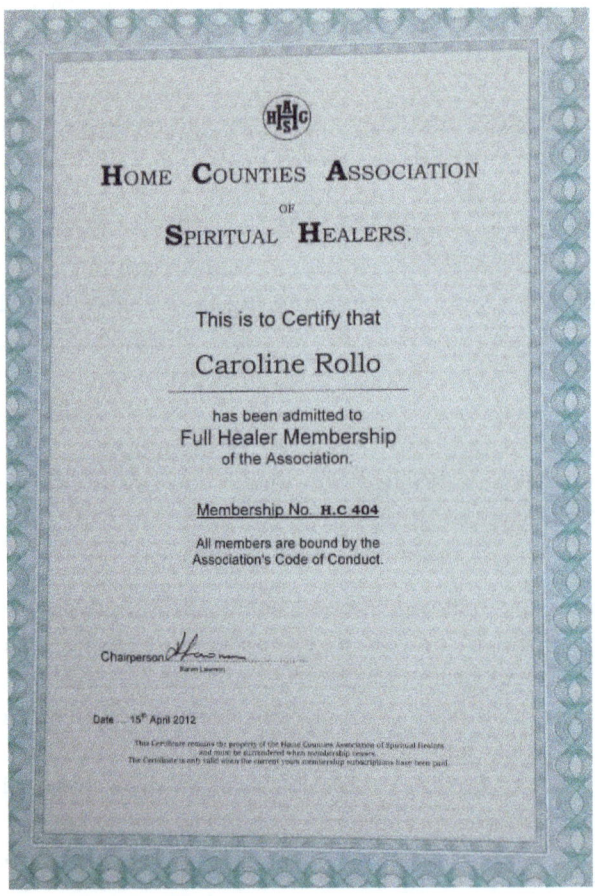

My certificate

Things known as Devils, Demons, Imps, Vampire energy's, ghoul, nightmare visitors, the banshee, Hags and shadow people who appear in a black mass, are troublesome demons and may need expulsion from your property or indeed a person, if they become a nuisance, you will need to get rid of such evil entireties found in or about your building, as these do have evil intent about them, even if it's just being mischievous Spirit these can cause stress and anxiety. Remember to be strong, you are the one in charge. Help however is always at hand, as a visit from a local medium would help you know what you are dealing with. They can do this by removing all bad energies from the building, smudging with white sage or Palo Santo Wood which is used widely with purification prayers and in some cases holy water is used.

And afterwards lavender in the rooms will help to calm and restore the good energy whilst getting back your home and calming things down, it's always a good idea to have your house blessed and I personally would close any open portals in the house and ask for it to remain in love and light. It may not be anything evil but may simply be a loved one that does not want to leave or a previous tenant who is residual going about their everyday business. Never attempt to cope with a situation alone without proper help, NEVER use a Ouija board as they are portals in many cases and can cause worse problems and things can go badly wrong by sometimes letting more bad spirits into your house via that board. In most cases it's very doable to resolve such a problem and things will soon get back to normal, like all things buildings and items hold energy and with that energy spirits can cling on to it. You may have bought something that has its own energy and history into your property without knowing of its history. If it's an item bought in, by removing that particular item the problems should cease.

I never believed in levitation until I first started out on this journey, I did not put my prayers of protection in place one evening as I popped into the spare bedroom and sat with my feet up on the bed doing meditations, I heard a rather silly giggle and got the sense of something running down the hallway, then saw in my meditation a pair of beautiful green eyes and the face of a fox, then found myself at the bottom on the bed. Not clever, do your homework.

If an unwelcome spirit attaches itself to you or a friend, it's known as a possession then and only then you bring in someone that can do an Exorcism, this will remove an evil spirits from a person's body or place by the use of prayer, expulsion of these demons is doable and then, purification of the person or place can be done, exorcism must be done by a professional. So, protecting yourself in love and light is very important. People have been known to dabble in this going on ghost hunts and taking it as a fun thing to do, then they find they become depressed and their moods change, it can be that they have an attachment.

Sleep Paralysis

This can sometimes happen and it is the strangest feeling as you are actually being pinned down in some way, unable to move. You may be relaxing in a chair on your own, or a lot of people experience waking up in bed and not being able to move. This is rare but I feel it needs to be mentioned, as it's quite common. If this should happen to you just remember the golden rule: your consciousness has to be strong, and it's ok to shout out in your head 'BACK OFF' I say in your head as speech is not always possible at this time when it's actually happening. This releases any hold they may have on you, but remember it may not be a bad Spirit but a loved one that has just drawn very close, too close into your personal space, but let them know it's uncomfortable and it will cease.

My Experience

I have had this happen several times to me personally, first time I seriously thought I was suffering a stroke, I was paralysed and could not move, I felt like I was sleeping on my tummy as I could not move forward, but then realised I was laying on my back, it did scare me at first, but when I learnt what it was, I got my head space right and shouted in my mind for them to back off and they did. It can happen with people who think it's a good idea to meditate in bed and they just fall asleep leaving themselves open to Spirit, your consciousness is not protected and you can allow other energies in, so bad idea.

Also, if you are in a meditation and wide awake and it get very black and dark with shadows, don't panic, picture a widow with the curtains drawn in your mind then pull back the curtains and see the light come flooding in, it does the trick and once more you have entered the love and light zone.

27
Working on Vibrations

Everything has its own vibration, different changes to our planet can alter these, but the spiritual wheels keep turning, by adapting to it and by adjusting our lives accordingly we are ok, it's very much up to us to adapt and harmonise. Vibrations can be felt from one person to another simply by shaking hands or having a hug. It is said that the same note from a violin played constantly on a certain vibration can destroy a bridge.

We aim for a pure clear mind, and we aim to be unbiased, and also to get our message across when our consciousness is totally in a neutral state for meditation, this will enable us to be in-tune with ourselves. When we have opened our third eye and our minds are open for learning new things, we can then be in tune with the earthly grids. We also learn to stop following the same old patterns and start to view things so very differently and approach things from different angles. We are unique, our very DNA says so. Mother earth talks to us on so many occasions through different vibrations all we have to do is listen.

The feeling is like when you hear a certain song on the radio, you are instantly on that vibration and all your emotions come to the front of your mind, a memory of a loved one or simply by listening to the vibration of the music giving you chills as it overwhelms your emotions. Meditating to Status Quo or head banging rock, it does not matter as long as it brings out your feelings, I love to play Italian tenor Andrea Bocelli, Questa Mia (This my Song) full blast its inspirational, it is sung in Italian so I am not concentrating on the words but the musical vibrations it brings.

28
One to One Readings

When learning to do this work you may wish to try reading for friends and family first it's always a good way to start and then you can progress through circle groups and begin to read for total stranger, perhaps doing their angel cards or trying one of the methods I have listed, whatever suits you best, as it's you that decide how you want to work, and no one else can do that for you, we are all unique. Just trust in what you receive and the way you receive it, are you sensing, seeing or hearing.

Working on Platform simply means standing up in front of an audience, whatever the venue, giving messages from the spirit world.. I had always been taught that there is a Beginning a Middle and an Ending to things, but in mediumship I reverse it.

The Ending for me is knowledge of how a person passed and The Middle is their memories to talk about and their lives, and their messages to pass on, and then there is The Beginning as for many relatives or friends need to understand it's their beginning to adapt without their loved one and carry on alone, and for the person who has died it's their beginning their new existence in love and light in spirit world.

When I get messages, I call it getting a link, and as I work, I can change gears into a better level of understanding, remembering it is not always easy for Spirit to come through. They make a great deal of effort, so it's up to me to listen and get it right. I would receive such odd messages for people at times and to translate them to a loved one was not always easy, I had to had to have the confidence in my own ability, if you get "No" I can't take that, move on, press forward keep asking questions in your head, spirit will give you the answers. Work according to your own potential. Try not to over think things just pass the information on that you receive. If you see something strange in your head, say it. If you start making it up you will get detached from what you are receiving and instead go with what you are personally thinking.

My Experience

I have done so many readings over the years, and to see people's joy when you have given a good message is a wonderful thing. When I am standing up in church I see so many faces staring at me all wanting that special loved one to come through with that special personal message, it can be difficult but I have tried not to be intimidated by this, just keeping calm and asking Spirit to kick in, they manage to point you in the right direction. I always found laughter helped at a service, if people are happy and relaxed you get a better atmosphere and better results.

If you go to see a medium for a one-to-one reading you should in theory, get a good reading. unless you are blocking for some reason, and that could be because you are just wanting a message too much, you're stressing and the feelings are tense which the medium will pick up on and the blocking occurs, just by you being over anxious. Also, if the atmosphere is down where you are working and you get too many negative reactions and feel like you yourself are being judged and tested, try to tell yourself in your head to push on and move forward. Most people soon realise when a medium is just cold reading you, and it can happen, you notice they are usually talking non stop, but getting no proof of the afterlife and no clear evidence for you.

Try to establish a good rapport with the person you are reading for, but if you cannot give any concrete evidence move on. Body language can be read, also facial expression, A medium needs to give basic evidence, a name, a situation or a memory. Remember it is not always the Mediums fault. If they are genuine, they will persevere and help you.

Routine to start working yourself

1. Go to spiritualist churches, circles and workshops.
2. Get into a routine of meditation.
3. Try to have your own spiritual time on a regular basis.
4. Set aside your time with Spirit when you will not be disturbed.
5. Decide on how you want to work. Or what works for you.
6. Read up on your particular way of working.
7. Get to know who your guides are just by asking.

8. Discover what Angels are around you personally. So you can call on them.//

9. Protection rules, know them off my heart as automatic kick ins.

10. Keep your consciousness strong, be the master of your own mind always.

Intuition

We all have Intuition in abundance. It is a natural ability to know and sense about a situation, when there is no evidence to support the fact. When you know or feel something is very wrong or when you find people acting in a certain way your intuitive gut kicks in. You hear the phone ring and you intuitively know who it will be before you answer. Everyone has this occasionally and it's an ability you can develop so it becomes even stronger. People in business for example use it as a guide to know when to make a good deal or whether to stand back and keep clear of a situation. Some people's intuition tells them when a loved one is unwell, or when they themselves are not quite right.

To strengthen your intuition, you can actually start listening and acting upon that little voice in your head that says what you're feeling at that time and you can have flashes of inspiration and pictures in your head. Mainly for me it's that gut feeling, from the yellow chakra, you know when things are wrong, you're stressed and you start to get that acidic tummy form. Spiritual Mediumship helps us to develop and increase the ability to sense. Meditation is definitely a technique to develop this, our hearts and mind connect to form gut feelings. Go with those feelings within you and run with them, they can serve you well.

Matrixing

I have been matrixing faces in things since I was a young girl. In my parents' bedroom at the cottage I would lay on their bed looking up at the ceiling where there were water stains from a leak in the roof and in these stains I would see so many faces looking down at me, and the old fashioned wooden headboard of theirs was full of eyes and faces and even today as I look at things I see faces all the time, it does not frighten me, as I am use to it now, bathroom tiles usually show me different faces in the stone tiles, and even folded towels can form a face. When reading for people at home I would see faces appear behind them in my plain grey sofa. I believe there are Spirit people amongst us all the time, as these faces come and go and even when looking at my garden they appear in tree trunks or bark, or in the wooden fencing or just clouds above. For me it's a wonderful feeling really that I am never alone, and I have never feared it. You might have had that experience yourself, it's really nothing to worry about, having experienced it all my life I just accept it. It is called Pareidolia and is a psychological phenomenon that causes people to see patterns in a random stimulus. This often leads to people assigning human characteristics to objects. Usually this is simplified to people seeing faces in objects where there really isn't one, but for a medium or spiritual person, it has a greater meaning.

29
My Meditations

When you first get into meditation you're eager and usually try too hard to communicate with Spirit. Meditation is the best way forward but don't sit there for hours trying too hard, just do it on at a regular time each day if you can, it is not a good idea to meditate in bed especially when you want to communicate with spirit and I would suggest when you first attempt this, always do it when you are wide awake sitting in a chair and be well-grounded with your feet firmly on the floor. Remember you are looking for colour, you are looking for images, maybe messages will pop into your head. Pictures and patterns, sometimes weird and wonderful stuff does happen. Do this at a time you won't be disturbed and feel totally relaxed. Whether you are meditating to music, or listening to a spiritual tape or as part of a circle group, put that Protection Prayer in place first. Manners cost nothing if you get something through to say thank you to Spirit, they will hear you.

To Start meditation control your breathing

From the start of any mediation the breathing has to be correct.

1. Sit in a comfortable position.
2. Lay your hands face up on your lap, so you are ready to receive.
3. Feet must be firmly on the ground, sense roots going from your feet into the floor giving you solid grounding.
4. Breath in the good air through your nose to the count of 4 Hold two seconds.
5. Breath out the bad through your mouth to the count of 4.
6. Do this breathing deeply for the first three or four times relaxing with each one.
7. Feel your shoulders going down as you breathe out.
8. Once you are relaxed in your chair you can begin to breathe slowly and steadily.

9. Pop your protection around you, open chakras. From the red base up to the crown.
10. Go on that journey or simply listen to music. Enjoy, no more than ten minutes to start.

Important: When opening your chakras remember say protection prayer first.

1. Open the red chakras first and work up.
2. Open crown chakra last, and only if you wish to connect to spirit.
3. Ask your gatekeeper to stand aside.
4. Ask Spirit Guides and helpers to come forward.
5. Allow at least 10 minutes from start to finish.
6. Build up gradually - I usually had 20 - 30 minutes eventually.

For Protection Prayer say:

Lord Father God, Mother Earth and Angels in the Universe please hear my prayer, (visualise the protection by placing your gold band of protection around yourself and your home and include loved ones if you like,) ask to be kept safe and in love and light when doing this. You may wish to open your chakras or just to balance them for yourself leaving the crown closed the meditation is yours, you may need just to take time out of a busy working day at work if our having a stressful day, just sit in the car or a private room and have that ten mins out to calm reset and relax.

Types of Meditations

Mediation to Try.

1. Relax into your chair and start the breathing.
2. Keep both feet firmly on the ground.
3. Breath in for the count of 4 through your nose.
4. Breath out for the count of 4 through your mouth.
5. As you breath out feel yourself sink into the chair and feel totally relaxed with steady normal breathing.

6. Stress will peel away as you concentrate just on your breathing control.
7. Hand on your lap face up ready to receive, Open chakras.
8. Imagine you're standing by a wooded area, see in your mind's eye the trees and greenery around you. Hear the birds singing and be ready to visualise walking along an upward footpath leading to a walled garden.
9. The sun is shining above your head and you are completely surrounded by love.
10. There are 10 large wooden steps in front of you, leading to a large oak gate.
11. Count in your head as you walk up the 10 steps.
12. Take hold of the large heavy iron latch on the oak gate and push the gate forward to open. Walk through and close the door behind you.
13. As you enter you will see a small pool of water with a tiny waterfall.
14. Walk forward, sit on one of two seats that are there placed together by the small pool.
15. Enjoy your time there asking questions in your head if you like.
16. See what comes forward and maybe if you have opened to Spirit, you may receive visitors, or have visions of gifts of knowledge of some sort.
17. Remain there until you are ready to go, a length of time that you are comfortable with.
18. Say thank you to Spirit, get up and visualise yourself walking back towards the gate, open it, walk through, then close it firmly behind you. Then walk down the 10 steps counting them as you descend. Back out of the wood Close the chakras and release the roots from your feet.
19. Feel your feet firmly on the ground and wiggle your toes.
20. When you're ready, open your eyes.
21. You should feel relaxed. Keep a journal of what you see.

Spiritual Knowings

The reason to keep notes in a journal at first of what you see is that you may realise who your guides are or receive some meaningful and relevant information for your everyday life at that moment in time. There are many different types of meditations, but if you can have that quiet time to take yourself to a familiar place and feel safe it can be rewarding. There are more stars out there in the universe than grains of sand on a beach, you will see weird and wonderful things, that's ok just allow yourself to feel the love. And getting a life balance again. Opening the third eye when getting to the brown chakra is totally optional. Your decision.

You will not get pictures through every time it may be just colour at first it is important to know, but on the occasion, you do, its magical and remember to try to keep a routine, don't sit for hours at a time thinking you will get more as it all happens gradually, I guarantee you will fall asleep if you do this too late at night, so do it when your wide awake and in control also if it is part of a daily or weekly routine build up from 10 minutes to about 20 minutes that's fine.

In any meditation you have to let your imagination fly, if you want to bring a loved one close to you, and to see them with the help of the third eye you can do this by letting your visualisation work for you, just imagine a loved one and see the shape of their heads and the smile on their face, see the tone of their skin, look at their eyes, their eyebrows, remember the colour and texture of their hair look at the shape of them and let your senses go round to their ears remember them, round to their mouth, is it smiling? Go down to their neck and then their body shape, breath in the perfume or aftershave they wore and see their hands. Familiar rings, did they smoke? Are they welcoming? You are bringing that person so near in a meditation, it can be quite wonderful. If it's a person or a place you wish to bring to the front of your thoughts you can, just let yourself be in that moment in time, you are totally safe, it's your head space.

You can access your best…

If you find it hard making personal decisions, spiritualism can make this process easier for you just by talking things over in your head and asking spirit to help, you do get the answers you're looking for. Loneliness can be terrible, so ask spirit to come forward and maybe bring new people into your life, make it happen and you can picture yourself in a better situation with a happier frame of mind, tell Spirit that is what you want to achieve. All people are struck by grief, or have some type of emotional turbulence at some point, so they need structure again to heal what has been broken. Spirit will help you cope and put things back in perspective, especially if you are getting addicted to things like drink, drugs, cigarettes or generally feeling out of zinc, Spirit will help by giving you direct access to a higher power for guidance, one day at a time is the key as you will once more level the unbalanced feelings, but like everything in life you have to ask and be clear about your intentions. Turning negatives into positives, words like I can't, become, I will and I can.

We all have quiet moments, we all have inner thoughts, just channel them for help, and receive the inner calm that's available, as all of your thoughts are always heard. When you are unable to do something physical to help the situation at least you can ask for help and healing in your mind and are left feeling better that at least you are doing something.

Spirit is the most dependable sauce of Love, it's unconditional, it makes you feel safe and gives you your worth. It will also help with doing anything that demands your creativity. Opening to spirit or simply being aware of this mass of energy that we can have access to knowing it can kick start and recharge our batteries. There is nothing wrong in focusing on ourselves for a change and asking for better things in life. If the results are positive, it can help the ones around us also, it's a win-win situation if you're in a happier place. It's not meditation all day, it's not praying all day, it's not even going to church, it's finding that inner peace, that awareness within ourselves, the knowing that we are not alone and we can be guided through life with a greater power at our side.

Private readings that affected me

I loved reading for people and always tried to make it a happy and positive experience, many people have such sad memories of a person suffering before their passing, and I completely understood how they were feeling, as they, like me, had found it hard to get past that thought of their loved one in pain. I would always try to explain about my Happy Box moment, you don't stop thinking about people when they die, so why can't you continue to talk about them in everyday life, it's because so many friends avoid the subject so they will not upset you. Whereas all you want to do is talk about them, it has helped me so much and a lot of people I read for. Remember, the Aura is so thin around you when you're sad, yet when you smile it expands out and glows up to twenty-five yards away from your body giving you that happy feeling and creating a warmth around you that enables Spirit to be close to you and your friends will find you more approachable.

I knew people needed evidence, especially something that was a personal memory to them. It may seem completely insignificant to you but to them it's everything.

An elderly lady from a local village came to see me. As soon as she got in the door I immediately said, 'May I ask who Bob is? her face went pink as she told me it was her husband and that he had just passed to Spirit a few weeks before, job done you may think, but I went on to tell her, that he loved cars, and how he was worried about her going up a ladder, she was shocked as she told me she had tried to get into the loft by herself that morning and it was too much for her. And how he had model cars up there. I then went on to give her things that popped into my head and her face just lit up, it was such a comfort to her to know she was not alone.

The most emotional readings for me are when someone had lost a child especially if it had been lost at a very young age, but the joy I see when a mother knows about a detail that I have given her, makes it all worthwhile, even babies that pass to Spirit can leave a message, as once they go back to Spirit, they are energy and can grow and get stronger, to be any age they wish to be.

Each reading given was taken seriously. I would always like people going home afterwards feeling better than when they came in. People are generally a little frightened of the unknown and death, and as we get older, we do think of this subject more. So, if you feel scared about passing to spirit, just turn your thoughts around and look at it as a wonderful new journey and new adventure.

People from all nationalities have come to me and somehow, I managed to get names in Italian, Indian German and French, Spanish and Polish, no language barrier at all. Also, I have seen people from all walks of life. In an array of occupations, and feel when it comes down to it, we are all the same, and we all have insecurities at times.

30
My Poetry

It has always been a passion of mine ever since I was little to try and write verse or some sort of poetry and even now if I am inspired when a loved one has a birthday, I like to put in a personal poem with the card, from my heart. working in churches my opening address were always something I had written, I think because I had to read these out loud to a lot of people, and I didn't have the anxiety about it, but was made more comfortable with words I had written myself, no word blindness, no panic, or that sick feeling I had experienced at school all those years ago, when asked to read in class in front of my school mates, in church as an adult all that panic just vanished.

I have enclosed just two for you to read, dyslexia may have hampered me but never stopped me. If you are an up and coming Medium then talk from the heart, that's all you need to do. I think one thing to remember when addressing people in churches you may have strong opinions on things but I would advise you to always listen to the other point of view. There are many things I have changed my mind on, over the years and that's a fact - I am not always right, and others are not always wrong, a balance has to be found.

Writing this book has been good for me as I wanted to share what I have experienced over the years and to let you know, if you have ever seen a UFO or had something weird and wonderful happen to you, it may be divinely given, don't be frightened to talk about it to others. The universe is mind blowing, wonderful and fathomless, but I strongly feel we are going to get our answers from vortexes of energy which will in turn lead us to these open portals with journeys to different worlds in different dimensions. We will not have to travel far to find them as they have been here all the time.

70 years on I look back and see the many challenges I have had to face, I have never been one to go off on long journeys or to be a great explorer and although I am quite well-travelled, I have been abroad many times on holidays, the places I have seen through the third eye, would blow your mind it cannot be explained to others, as you yourself have to be in

the moment, I will look forward in the next life to continue with this everlasting spiritual journey.

I want to share with you two of my poems that I have used as addresses for church services in the past.

This one is dedicated to all those people who run spiritual churches up and down the country. They keep the spiritual doors open, for very little thanks at times going out in all weathers, they do work extremely hard, and give a strong meaning to the community.

You Don't Have to be a Medium

You don't have to be a medium
To work for Spirit, I'm sure
You may just be the person
Who keeps open the spiritual door
You might be the person
Who books the hall each week
Inviting different mediums
To come along and speak

You don't have to be a medium
To work for Spirit, I know
You might be the one who makes the tea
Or the kind person that clears up the hall, when others go

Every week without fail, those doors are open wide
Mediums are booked and telephoned just to provide
A link with the other side, A link with Spirit divine
No, you don't have to be a Medium, to be given a sign

Spirit works in wonderful ways
And choose the generous of heart
People who don't get all the glory
But who are there, from the very start

For without this dedication
Many of us would fall
People need the knowledge that life goes on
To remember and recall
I can provide the messages
As Spirit gives them to me
But without the help of others
I dread to think where we would be

Thank you, kind people, who run a spiritual church
For keeping the doors open wide.
As it's through, sunshine, rain, thunder and snow
They do this job with pride...

- Caroline Rollo (20.5.2014)

Caroline Rollo

I wrote this next poem at Easter as it is a special time for me. I suppose it is the great feeling about coming from darkness into the light which has helped me overcome difficult times. I decided to have both of my sons Christened at Easter for this very reason the service started at 9pm in the evening, the venue was Priory Church Dunstable, Bedfordshire. People rang me to ask if they had misread the invitation, I said No it's right. 9 pm. When they arrived, the church was all in darkness, they then gave a candle to everyone to hold and one person lit a candle from the back of the church until the whole church was filled with candle light, it was so beautiful and such a wonderful service. It inspired my next poem.

Candles

A candle is a living symbol
A sign of hope for all
When the love light flickers,
Against the darkest wall

At Christmas we have advent
Four, to be lit in turn
For Peace, Hope, Love and Joy
We need to see them burn

As they flicker and flare up
We are sharing our prayers in love
And all our thoughts and prayers are heard
By The Divine Spirit above

I light mine to remember my Mum and Dad
And my other loved ones, who have passed
It's a prayer sent in love and light
And a connection with Spirit at last

So next time you light your candle
Take time to stop and stare
It's not just an action, to bring forward the Light
It's a very special prayer

- Caroline Rollo (21.12.2013)

If you have read this book and get something from it, I have achieved my aim which is to help would- be Mediums or people who simply want to know more about spirit world and spiritual connections. I know we all have a natural ability to get the very best out of ourselves just by sensing and feeling the energy around us, being in our own personal space is important and being in a happy place and safe bubble in our mind enables us to control the ever-moving energies within our own body. As we create good energy within ourselves, we actually pass it onto others. People who can motivate us are inspirational, and they have this spiritual energy in abundance, our perception on life changes so much, our cup is no longer half empty but half full once more. How many of us actually get up and say in our heads thank you for another day, thank you for the hot shower, thank you for a hot meal, thank you for a comfortable bed, as in the blink of an eye these things can be taken away. Everyone will have issues of stress at times and depression, and everyone usually hides it well. A gift of a simple smile, or a listening ear can help so much when others are struggling. This beautiful mother earth of ours is sitting on a giant magnet, levitation defies gravity, yet in some place's things do levitate, such as stones and even plants are affected. What wonders have we yet to discover.

I hope you enjoyed the book, and my ramblings, if indeed you ever want to go down the route of being a medium, or just a more, spiritual person, I can only say it's been the best experience of my life, not only does it take away any fear of death it has given me faith and understanding that life indeed does go on. We all need to believe in something, to carry us through life's ups and downs and by believing in spirit it has not only carried me through life's difficult times but also given me that extra love and guidance by a greater power and has always given me the strong evidence that there is indeed more.

31
Finally

I have always agreed with the saying it is better to walk with a friend down a road, rather than to ride in a carriage alone, sharing worries thoughts and feeling with friends or even a complete stranger is important especially for our mental health, love is out there, we just have to trust and have a little faith. Spirits will give us guidance and love, as it's there for all to connect to. You are Never Alone, it's just a knowing.

Thank you to my husband John my life's companion
who has stood by me in all my ups and downs.

Thank you to my sons David and Ian,
who helped me when I lost my way in life.

Thank you to my Family and my Friends
for their love and support.

Special thanks to Roy Cowley who encouraged me
and supported me in this project.

This book was written for my beautiful grandchildren
and to help would-be Mediums or people who want to
know more about the world of Spirit.

The author outside Harrods, London in 2000

Whatever our roadmap in life may be, or wherever our path should take us, be assured. Spirit will always walk beside us, we are never alone

*Available worldwide online
and from all good bookstores*

www.mtp.agency

@mtp_agency

www.ingramcontent.com/pod-product-compliance
Lightning Source LLC
LaVergne TN
LVHW011703050325
805087LV00011B/990